The White Eagle Book
of Healing Meditations

THE WHITE EAGLE BOOK OF HEALING MEDITATIONS

White Eagle

Meditations and Contemplative Teaching
with the photographs of Werner Achermann

THE WHITE EAGLE PUBLISHING TRUST
NEW LANDS · LISS · HAMPSHIRE · ENGLAND · GU33 7HY

First published September 2008

© Copyright, The White Eagle Publishing Trust, 2008
Illustrations © Copyright, The Estate of Werner Achermann, 2008

British Library Cataloguing-in-Publication Data
A catalogue record for this book is available from the British Library

ISBN 978-0-85487-199-5

Set in Lydian and Goudy Sans at the Publisher and
Printed in Great Britain by Cambridge University Press

CONTENTS

INTRODUCTION

IT IS hoped that the passages in this book will be continually useful in a variety of circumstances: encouraging to those who feel in need of support and comfort, and helpful to those who wish to raise their consciousness and become more receptive to healing. They have been chosen also to be supportive to those caring for others, as well as inspiring to healers and to those who wish to understand their inner natures. No previous knowledge of meditation is necessary since the meditative passages carry one 'upwards' through the love and power of the words alone. White Eagle's meditations are so uplifting and gentle that healing occurs simply through reading them. They bring close the essence of divine love.

White Eagle says that true healing comes from making contact with the Christ. By Christ he does not mean the personality of Jesus, but rather the Christ spirit—the essence of divine love. He also means the light that is at the heart of each one of us and makes us, too, sons and daughters of God. When we are able to touch that divine essence with openness and surrender, the power of our connection to the Father–Mother is stimulated, and the Christ spirit—which White Eagle often simply calls the Light—within each one arises to take control of the body once more. Thus all parts of the self—from the soul to the physical form—can be returned to harmony, can come back into balance. In this way so-called miracles can occur, and do occur at a soul level. This book is intended to help the individual make that inner connection, to allow healing to take place.

Healing, both of the individual and generally, is central to the White Eagle work. The majority of the teaching and the meditations in this book have been given during services of rededication for White Eagle healers, and healing services for those in need. During these services White Eagle has been able to convey great love and compassion, and deep understanding for the needs of all. Through that deep compassion and inspiration, healers are able to reconnect with the divine love that they seek to channel for their patients and with the constructive, positive thought which enables them to continue in their work. Moreover, those in need of healing are able to touch a level of consciousness at which healing can occur. They may also understand how healing works, and what they can do to help themselves receive and benefit from it.

*

The book is divided into sections, each with a passage for contemplation and a meditation. It is hoped that the passages for contemplation will bring the kind of understanding to the mind that enables it to let go preconceptions about the self—to understand the source of healing and to surrender to the inner will.

At the beginning of each meditation a significant phrase from the contemplative passage is repeated as a reminder of the theme. After this, there are a few words intended to help the reader attune to the White Eagle

meditation that follows. The meditations then enable the reader to reach a level of peace, stillness and awareness, where the higher self can take charge and healing can begin to occur. The meditative passages can be used either as meditations in themselves, or as visualizations upon which the reader can reflect.

Contemplations and meditations alike can have a wide range of applications among both individuals and groups. A person wishing to make contact with the source of healing may use either the contemplations or meditations as a daily means of tuning in to the source or as a means of becoming more peaceful and positive in order that the body can heal itself. The meditations can be used by group leaders who may wish to help their group rise in consciousness, and may be just right for reading to a person in hospital or to someone unable to read for themselves.

In this book, you will become familiar with recurring images such as 'the temple of healing' and 'the blue lake', and concepts such as the guardian angel. But one that White Eagle uses again and again is 'the Star'. Like anything connected with the imagination, the six-pointed Star (which can be pictured in either two or three dimensions) can be regarded from many different points of view and given a vast range of meanings. What White Eagle most simply intends to convey is the light within that represents our link with God, the whole spiritual world, and the whole of time from the very birth of life. Therefore it represents an ideal and is a symbol of our perfection. Perfection means our total healing at all levels of life, not just the physical. White Eagle would say that the very act of focusing on the Star has the effect of bringing our atoms into alignment. Sometimes he calls it 'the Christ Star': on these occasions, it means exactly the same as 'the Christ' in the way in which that concept was defined earlier.

The accompanying CD contains a selection of White Eagle meditations from the book. These meditations are read in such a way as to be creative and real, as if one were being led in a meditation group. They were taken down just as White Eagle gave them and therefore are slightly adapted from the originals. Each meditation is interspersed with short, specially-created pieces of harmonious sound.

Werner Achermann's photographs are intended to give the book imaginative breadth and open the imagination. Werner was a member of the White Eagle work in Switzerland until he passed into spirit in 1984. Most of the photographs were taken in the last ten years of his life. In using them we salute a dear friend of White Eagle and remember with love his wife Elsi too.

Through White Eagle's uplifting presence may you feel above all that there is hope: not just individually, but for the world. May you receive healing and be yourself a healer for others.

I.
Sounding the Word of God

WE WANT you to understand that through your mind and in your meditations every day you can utilize *the substance that is called 'light'*. Indeed, you are already utilizing it by taking it and moulding it in your bodies. How can you become more conscious of your work with the light? We stress again the truth that you are masons, you are builders, and your building material is soul-substance and light. This light can be realized *in you*. All visible creation is light in form. Every form of matter is fundamentally light. All life is vibration, and according to the quality or rate of vibration the light takes differing forms. How are you to commence working as a builder? Already there are many who are doing it unconsciously.

People are satisfied to live an ordinary good life, during which they suffer some pain and many disabilities. It seems almost as though every soul is heir to disease and death. We would suggest that the 'normal' life, however well-lived, falls short somewhere, although it goes a certain way. So consciousness of the reality of what you are doing has to be brought through. What must happen in every soul is an awakening to the truth that God is light, and that you are light; and that you have been given working tools with which to build your temple of light. These working tools are your body, your emotions, your thoughts—physical, astral, mental. You will have to learn to use these tools if you want to build your temple. Then, when in due course you have graduated, you will appear as beautiful and perfect as that jewel of the master soul.

In your meditations, try to conceive this ideal of the flashing golden jewel. Within that jewel—or shall we call it the six-pointed Star?—is to be seen the perfect form of man or woman. This perfect form is the perfected son–daughter of God. This is you! This is also your ideal.

To work with the light you need to withdraw your consciousness, your thoughts and your emotions from the outer world. You must turn to the inner world, the home of spirit. Within this world of stillness, which constitutes the centre and the source from which all outward form and outward life proceed, you will attune yourself to the one tremendous note, which we will call the 'Word' of God. *In the beginning was the Word and the Word was with God. God is Light. The Word was God.* Turn within, closing all the senses of the body. In silence the Word can be still heard. That Word is the first cause of life. It is the vibration of that Word which you would hear. This is what the aspirants seek who withdraw from the world. They go into the snowclad peaks to meditate and to hear the Word.

The sound nearest to that Word that it is possible for men and women to comprehend is the hum of creative life, which is interpreted as *Aum*. Those who know how to sound that Word can feel the vibration of life quickening them as they sound it, can feel the seed-atom of God within the heart. By so doing they are releasing that life and light within.

'Those who know how to sound that Word can feel the vibration of life quickening them as they sound, can feel the seed-atom of God within the heart. By so doing they are releasing that life and light within.'

Sound can be a particularly strong way to enter meditation and to be in touch with the creative power of God. Listen to some music that you like before you begin to meditate. Focus on one sound or the melody that best opens your heart and raises your feelings beyond those of everyday. When it is finished, expand your awareness into the silence that comes after, as if you were following that sound into the inner world of your being—or into the cosmos.

Meditation: A GOLDEN TEMPLE

COME WITH us just for a brief moment or two. Come with us right up into that golden world, that heaven world, to feel the warmth of the Son, or sun. Can you bask in this Sun and be bathed in it? Can you feel the life-force of the Sun?—not burning you, but healing you, and bringing to your heart happiness and joy in your reunion with spirit.

The Christ presence is drawing us, and we follow him. The Christ draws us all into the golden temple of healing. See this temple: use your creative power, your imagination. See it, feel it, follow him right into this golden temple where all the rays, all the colours in the Christ Light, are actively giving you life, giving power, giving you health, giving you strength to carry on all through your journey of life.

We are in this golden temple, a building of the most perfect, gentle and exact architecture. See the grand pillars supporting the archways. Feel the power in this temple of the Spirit. We stand together shoulder to shoulder, hand in hand, and we listen to the harmony of heaven, to the harmony of life. And we listen to the Great Word of God, that grand and glorious *Aum*.

You are in it. Life is all around us, eternal, glorious, perfect. He who is the Grand Master of all stands before the golden blazing altar, holding in his hand the holy grail cup, the human heart ... *his* heart. And you find that he is standing before you, and the golden cup of golden wine passes from his lips to yours. Drink: drink this golden essence with his love, divine love. Accept, accept it and be filled, my child, and you will feel an ecstasy and a joy unknown on earth. You will feel the vibrations, the life-force, all around you and in you, and working through you. This is heaven.

2.
The Healing Power of the Light

IN ORDER to receive the true healing power, it is well for the soul to be attuned to the infinite light and love, which every soul is capable of doing. We know the heaviness and weariness of the flesh, but the flesh is only heavy and weary when darkness creeps in. Darkness comes in many ways and one of the chief ways is over-stress and strain, anxiety and fear in the life.

When you can attune yourselves, when you can centre your whole thought upon the spirit of the Lord Christ, the gentle master, you will find the weariness of the flesh will fall from you because, by your own inner effort, you are transmuting those dark atoms into light. You will feel light, you will feel light-hearted, and you will feel at peace. You will realize that there is a power superior to your own which raises you from darkness and heaviness and weariness into a state of lightness and confidence. You will know that you are in the care of the wise, loving Father–Mother God.

We know that this sounds simple and childlike, but the Master Jesus himself came to tell the world this simple truth. And he said, or at least the Christ light through him said, *I am the way, the truth and the life.* 'I AM' … which is the light within the human soul. Very often it is a small light that is covered up, but as the soul becomes more aware, that light shines forth with great power. In those of you who are weary and sick, it is only the lack of experience in bringing into operation this light that causes ill health.

To be healed spiritually means that the spirit is able to fill the physical body and the soul body with light. If you could see with your inner vision when a healer was at work, and if the healer was very strong spiritually, you would see light coming from his or her finger tips, and radiating from the whole body. This light is the instrument of the healing power and it is generated by love, or what we describe as the spirit of Christ or the spiritual Sun. The spiritual Sun is the Christ spirit, the divine essence, which is the source of all life. It is life itself.

Whatever your disease, whatever your distress or your problem, try to forget your symptoms (although we know this is hard), and visualize the light as though you were looking right into the heart of the Sun. Imagine you are doing this and try to understand that your true self is a body of radiant light: glorious, brilliant light. This is the body that is wholly healthy, and it is the body which you will in due time inhabit, when you have discarded the denseness of earth. But you do not have to wait until you leave the physical body because you can, even while here on earth, cause this body of light to manifest through your physical body. When it does so all disease departs because you are then in a state of absolute and perfect harmony.

It is for you to work for yourselves to realize this divine power in your innermost heart. Try not to think of disease, or of dis-ease; concentrate on harmony, light. If it were possible for you all to live consciously in this light all the time, you would need no healing from outside. The light would heal you.

Keep striving towards the light. Each time you fall back into the darkness, rise again into thoughts of joy and light and beauty. You are not only here to feed and clothe your bodies. You are here for a grander purpose than that: to develop those spiritual qualities and powers that will enable you to enter in fullness into the beauty of God's life.

'There is a power superior to your own which raises you from darkness and heaviness and weariness into a state of lightness and confidence.'

Our guardian angel helps us raise our consciousness from the heaviness of earthly concerns to the confidence of the presence of God, both in and with us. The angel may indeed be the principal agent of that 'power superior to your own'. As we follow the meditation opposite, taking the path of light into the heart of the Christ Star enables our angel to draw close, and so raise us further. Try not to worry too much whether what you see is 'all in your mind' but use your imagination to see the pathway before you. As you become more and more focused, feel the presence of a being with you to whom you are very precious. That feeling of divine love, beyond earthly emotion, will transcend all boundaries and allow your loved ones in spirit to draw close to you.

Meditation: GUARDIAN ANGEL

AS WE raise our consciousness, we see before us a pathway of light. As we follow the path of light we are drawn upwards, into the blazing six-pointed Star.

We are bathed in the pure, life-giving rays of the Christ Star. Peacefully we breathe in the light and feel it flowing through every cell of our being, releasing all frets and tensions of the outer self. We are becoming still in the Star. Strong rays enfold us in wings of light as our guardian angel draws close to our inner most being.

We become more still, more peaceful, as deep in the heart a clear flame arises, grows and illumines our whole consciousness with a quality of God, divine peace, strength, courage, heavenly wisdom, joy, love.

The angel's wings raise us heavenwards and we are bathed, immersed, irradiated with that God-quality which we need, deep within our soul. Right now, become aware of the beautiful garden of reunion. Stay here a while and commune with your loved ones.

3.
Light is the Life-force

THE LIFE or light-force coursing through your veins is the secret of perfect health. Yes, lack of light leads to lack of certain elements in the bloodstream. This can cause a breakdown in health of the physical body. Jesus knew how to command the light, how to receive the radiation of the Sun of God. He did not need to *touch* a sick person to send light into that body, for he had also overcome limitations of time and space. Do you remember the miracle of the man who came to Jesus begging that his servant might be healed? Jesus replied, 'He is healed already'. The Christ-consciousness within Jesus caused his aura to expand and reach to the sick man, infusing him with the vibrations of light, bringing light into darkness.

Light is the very life of God. It brings life to the physical body; it brings eternal life to the soul. So the object of your being is to discover and to use this secret so as to become a true and perfect light or son–daughter of God. You may think that you, personally, have a long way to go? Yes, so have we all.

Dear ones, be patient; do not look back over your shoulders. Turn your faces to the light and keep on keeping on trustingly and patiently. Be encouraged, not disappointed. If you are sad or suffering, may you receive a demonstration of God's love and its power to work miracles in the body and material life. It is the law: God has so created sons and daughters that they must themselves release the light before it can act in them, and also in their circumstances and their material conditions.

So, look to the light. The light shall overcome all darkness and set you free. Freedom means peace of soul, happiness, joy abounding, and abundance of all needful things. Yes, humanity is approaching the time when it will be able to command for the good of all the action of the light in matter.

What is love? Understand that love is life; it is light, it is holiness, healthfulness. For when a person loves—that is, with the divine love—the whole being becomes illumined. Since this love is light, this is the power of all healing.

'Do you remember the miracle of the man who came to Jesus begging that his servant might be healed? Jesus replied, "He is healed already". The Christ-consciousness within Jesus caused his aura to expand and reach to the sick man, infusing him with the vibrations of light, bringing light into darkness.'

The Light, or Christ, was embodied in the Great Healer, Jesus. That presence is always there when healing is taking place. In the following meditation his aura expands through time and space to bring you healing. It is through the awareness of light at the inner level that we begin to expand in consciousness. Begin by imagining that you are sitting in a pool of light or a spotlight and that the light is not only around you, but penetrates every cell of your being.

Meditation: BREATHING IN THE LIGHT

AS WE attune our hearts in love and devotion to the Christ Presence, we can be quite sure that we shall meet the Christ at the spiritual level of consciousness.

Try, if you can, to forget the material life, and think only of the spiritual temple of light. We are gathered in this temple of light, and the light is the life of God, the spiritual life and the power. As it pours into your waiting consciousness it will cleanse and purify you on the three levels of consciousness—the physical level, the soul level, and the spiritual level.

In this temple of light there is a pool of water. We call it water, but it is water charged with spiritual force, like electric force; and you are taken through this pool of water. Visualize this scene and the healers in their white robes gently taking their patients through this healing, cleansing water. Go through it yourself, and you will feel the cleansing of your body at all levels. The water will not wet you, rather it will cleanse you....

Now we pass from this healing pool out through the arch of the temple doors, into the sunlit gardens. You may see the flowers in profusion. We walk through the gardens until we come to a fountain of light. Visualize this fountain of sparkling light, tiny sparks of light. Go right into this fountain and let these tiny sparks of light pour over you and recharge you. Breathe in slowly and steadily....

Breathe out....

Keep on breathing in this light, breathe it in ... and breathe it out....

Now every atom of your body is charged with this light, which is perfect life....

Within you, in your heart chakra, is the permanent life-cell. From this permanent life-cell your whole being can be recreated and recharged. When you make your contact with the presence of the Lord Christ, you are receiving into your heart chakra his light and life, and through your heart and that permanent life-cell, it will recreate you.

4.
Natural Healing comes from the Heart

WHEN A healer who has a degree of spiritual healing power puts forth his or her hand to heal, there flows from that hand a light, an emanation, which sometimes extends beyond the fingers for two or three inches. When this hand treats the patient these etheric fingers seem to penetrate the body of the sufferer. This, of course, is dependent on the development of spiritual power in the healer. The power we describe comes from the creative centre of a person's being and rises up through the body. When fully developed and controlled it causes a very beautiful aura or illumination to project from the man or woman. One who has arrived at that degree of spiritual healing power can be called an initiate.

The central chakra is at the heart. When this power is consciously released in the individual it should go forth in love from the heart. Indeed this power *must* go through the heart for safe use; it *must* go forth as Jesus the Christ directed, in great compassion, in selfless love. We will go so far as to say that all people who have developed the heart chakra and love all beings, love animals, love nature, and love to give out love, are natural healers giving the most vital power that can be given to the world.

When your heart is full of love and compassion you are sending out from your own centre the light which God has implanted in you as a tiny seed, a seed that is growing all the time. As you aspire to the Great White Spirit, so this light and power is growing in you. Every thought of God, every prayer to God, every small effort that you make to think rightly—to convey to all beings truth and purity, to reach up to the higher level of harmony, love, purity and goodness—is helping to heal the whole world. Spiritual healing is healing the sick soul of the world, the sick soul of a country or a nation and the sick souls of men and women. To heal sick bodies is good, but to heal the soul is better. This manifestation of sunlight through you, the quiet infiltration of this holy light into people's hearts and lives, will heal the whole world.

'We will go so far as to say that all people who have developed the heart chakra and love all beings, love animals, love nature, and love to give out love, are natural healers giving the most vital power that can be given to the world.'

Jesus once talked about the eternal spring of God's light and love. In this meditation you are helped to contact that eternal spring as a fountain of living water which can bring healing not only to yourself, but to the whole world. To begin, think of the physical qualities of water and how devastating is the lack of it. You can bring soul healing to the world as a stream of water arising in a parched desert. Focus in your heart centre on love for humanity and its need for light.

Meditation: THE FOUNTAIN OF LIGHT

WE ASK you to see with your inner vision a beautiful fountain. It is rising from the earth, shining in the light of the Star above; and the rays of the Star and these streams of water from the fountain are pouring down, cleansing us, enfolding us. The light is dancing on the falling water; it is almost like gems of water. You are able to go to the very heart of the fountain. Feel that you are part of this fountain of light—cool, cleansing, and powerful—but powerful in a very peaceful, beautiful way. Let us, for a few moments, become part of this fountain of light, of pure water, of spiritual power....

We are in the garden in the world of light. You can drink the water.... Do you see how the angels and indeed the spirits of the water, of the water element, are all part of this great fountain, as we are?

And now there is a very beautiful feeling, an understanding that we are able to take a chalice of water, and carry it to those who are thirsting, thirsting for the living waters....

Come back now to the centre, where the brethren are gathered, and be aware of the presence of our Master. He touches the heart. This is to strengthen you in your healing work.

The touch is given with great love, but it is also a call

to service: a prayer that always in your work you shall consciously rise in spirit and join the brethren gathered in the temple above, round the central altar, all lifting their hearts to the great Sun, and enfolded in the love of Divine Mother, giving us power to create beauty, peace and truth on earth.

5.
Surroun-ded by Angels

WHEN YOU wish to heal the sick, or comfort a troubled one, you need to concentrate your whole being upon God, your Creator. Remember the words of Jesus, *I and my Father are One*. It is so important not to take too much notice of the noisy things in life. Withdraw from them; if you can go into your own sanctuary it will be easier. When you are in the world it is more difficult to withdraw from noise, but try to do this.

As soon as you enter the temple of your own being, where it is quiet and harmonious and beautiful, you immediately open your heart to God. And you feel the love of God, and the power of God, not only flowing into you, but rising within you and flowing out to meet the encircling band of angels.

You are surrounded by angels. You may not be able to see them, but you may be able to feel them. They are with you, in the quiet of your own innermost being. Maybe you are unconscious of it, but something is happening on the etheric plane of life. And when your clairvoyance or your clear vision is open, you will see the formation of the rays of light. You will see them not only flowing to you, but flowing from you, often creating form. But, you are not concerned with seeing anything while you are healing. You are only concerned with what you are feeling in your heart, towards God and all creation.

Love, love much, for there is nothing which God has not created. Love all, because there is nothing God has ever hated.

This is the secret of all healing and to those who ask to learn how to heal. We say, learn to love—love. Feel love in your heart towards

God first and to life and to nature. Cultivate love, compassion, sympathy. Acknowledge that life is governed by law and the law is God! Separate yourself from the law, and suffering enters in. Because there are these cross-currents in your life and in your work, hold fast, dear healers, to this simple feeling of love; and then you will get that feeling of love in your life, particularly through the world of nature.

'You are surrounded by angels. You may not be able to see them, but you may be able to feel them. They are with you, in the quiet of your own innermost being.'

The angels bring all the qualities needed for healing. They are God's agents in creation of all form. They bring a sweetness and joy that is beyond all earthly sensation. To begin the meditation overleaf, imagine a time when you have felt creative, or created something—it doesn't matter how mundane that thing might be. Feel the sense of bringing something into being which was never there before: a lovely bed of flowers, a meal for your friends, a poem, picture or dance. Nurture that creative vibration and allow it to build within you.

Meditation: ON WINGS OF LIGHT

WE ARE going to leave behind the physical body, and in our higher minds we are going to see and enter the temple of spiritual healing. This is the temple that holds the creative power of God, the power that recreates. You must see and contact this power in your individual healing work, for you have to get into the mind of God and create, *create* perfection.

Now here we see the great canopy of white wings. They are alive—they are living wings, pulsating wings, pulsating with light over all this shrine, this temple in the spirit world. We are right up on the mountaintop, and the air we breathe is pure and fresh. As we enter the portals of this temple, on either side, like two pillars, stand two angels. As we pass them, we are offered the cup of pure water, the grail cup. Sip, sip the water of life, the healing water, and enter this holy place....

Now we are in a golden world, and we see all round in a circle these angel forms with wings of light, beautiful faces: all so perfectly peaceful and joyous. You can feel the joy. You can feel the peace, and feel your troubles and your heaviness all falling away. We look about us, and see that the dome of wings is supported by tall pillars of light, and each pillar is a great healing angel. Oh, we feel ... we feel this power, this healing, this lovely, beautiful blessing. All is quiet, and the souls of the sick are brought in. They are sleeping: they know not where they are, but we are able to see the angels healing them. This is where they are brought when you are doing your healing work. Never doubt this. If you are true to God and yourself, you are taking part in a true ceremony, a true service of healing. You will hear the music, the harmony. You will inhale the sweetness of the heavenly essence. We have no words with which to describe the fragrance in the healing temple.

The Great Healer now is walking among you, smiling into the face of each one of you, touching you, blessing you. Just be true to your spirit in your heart, and you will know God, and God's love and God's work. The Great Healer is saying to us all in the healing temple: 'Return, my children, recharged with this heavenly power, and may peace and joy remain ever in your heart'.

6.
The Healing Power of Music

WE NOW speak of music, and you will wonder what connection there is between music and healing. One of the most prized and, shall we say, coveted spiritual gifts is that of healing. Now there are many forms of healing. Not only the laying-on of hands—that is one form. Not only the projection of rays of light and colour—that is another. Not only magnetic or nature healing. There is also the healing power of music. In the world of spirit, many souls need healing when they first arrive from a chaotic physical life. Such souls are gently carried to the clinics or the temples of healing, and there they are surrounded by beauty and hear music according to their soul's need. Beauty is of God and is important in spiritual healing and unfoldment; sincerity and simplicity are also of great assistance in spiritual unfoldment, but beauty one might liken to the bridal garment of heaven. Beauty is an aspect of God, and through beauty the soul is raised to a consciousness of the presence of God.

Now there is nothing like harmonious music for creating harmony in a person's soul. Sound and music provoke feeling; through feeling and imagination you develop gifts of the spirit, yet feeling and imagination are the very qualities so many human beings lack. This is why beautiful music is almost a necessity in spiritual work—it can contribute to the awakening and development of a person's feeling for God, feelings of Christ's presence. The Christ qualities in the human soul are awakened when it hears beautiful sound. Moreover, as the sound is sent forth from the instrument you should be able to see very beautiful colours emerging. The colours are created from the sound of beautiful and harmonious music: strong and powerful when the music is strong and powerful; soft and gentle when the music is quiet. You may even see the vibrations from sounds, out of which is created a heavenly temple.

Each one of you has a predominating note, according to the predominating planetary influence in your soul. This means that in your aura you have a predominating colour, for every note is expressed by a colour. Every planetary vibration is a colour. The combination of the seven notes of music, the seven colours of the spectrum, brings into being the one grand harmony, the one divine Light, which is the Light of Christ—Love. Love, then, contains all. Love contains wisdom and power. In the Trinity we find the one predominating note; but if you know perfect love, you know wisdom; if you have wisdom and love, you are powerful and have poise. The three qualities are inseparable. Three in One, One in Three is the divine fundamental note of music, of the harmony of life....

'The combination of the seven notes of music, the seven colours of the spectrum, brings into being the one grand harmony, the one divine Light, which is the Light of Christ—Love.'

Colour, sound and scent all play a part in healing—in bringing harmony to the soul and right through into the physical body and mind. When healing is needed, the angels will bring to the appropriate chakra the colour needed to maintain the overall harmony. As you are reading this, you may already be feeling drawn to a colour or colours that you need at this moment. Allow your mind to be still, unattached, so that as you rest the chakra can be receptive.

Meditation: THE SEVEN RAYS

IMAGINE a beautiful temple, set in the midst of exquisite scenery—green meadows, banks of flowers—an open temple with seven pillars supporting the domed roof, with its interior full of light and of the most beautiful, soft, almost indistinguishable colours.

The roof is open to the white light, which contains within its ray all the seven colours of the rainbow, but so beautifully blended together that they seem just one great white light. Green seems to be the foundation, or the harmonizing colour—beautiful green grass beside banks of flowers: all the various shades of colour.

On the daïs in the centre of this temple is the Shining One, who is to conduct not an orchestra as you know it but one invisible. When this shining figure raises his rod of power, or baton, there is a tuning-in of this invisible orchestra.

All around, on grassy slopes or mossy beds, are patients, some not yet released from their physical bodies, still living on earth, but brought during the time they are asleep—very often put gently to sleep so that they can be released from the physical body.

Then the rod of power is raised, and the tuning-in note sounded; and the gentle harmony of the orchestra gradually swells, and colours seem to flow from the baton, from the rod of power—more beautiful colours than you can ever see. The colours are directed to the patients, and as the patients listen, the psychic centre that needs the particular ray of power absorbs it. In many cases all the sacred centres of the body are opened to absorb these beautiful colours, which are yet notes of music and harmony created by the direction, or the will, of the Shining One.

Some are thus healed; and many of you can find healing. Call upon White Eagle to help you, and White Eagle comes, as you go to sleep. Be still … listen … and receive….

7.
There is Purpose in Suffering

YOU MAY be sad because of the sufferings of those you love. It is very hard to have to remain still, to be unable to do anything.

Whenever you witness suffering of the body or of the mind which you are unable to heal, try to remember that the sufferer is working through a condition of life which will eventually bring the soul into the light. So it is your work ever to hold your beloved friend or dear one that light, that hope, that courage, which will help his or her soul make good. We assure you that what we call the Great White Spirit is a God of infinite love and tenderness. And every child of God is ordained to go through experiences on earth that will bring it into the happiness and peace for which it longs.

We give you this message as one of hope, and to comfort you. For what takes place in the personal life, in the individual and particular life, is taking place too in the collective life. That which you see in the world, which appears painful, is the way that the race must travel. That which you see in the personal suffering of someone is the way that that particular soul must travel until healing comes. It is not easy at first to trust, and to hold fast to the inner light and truth of the heart. The body seems so solid, heavy and intractable and the mind so wayward. But the mind must become the tool of the spirit, and the substance of the body can be lightened, refined and uplifted by aspiration and by your love and devotion to God.

This constant dwelling in the presence of God will come to mean more to you than anything else in your life. *Seek ye first the kingdom of God ... and all these things shall be added unto you.* Divine

Intelligence is just, perfect and true, and can make no mistake, but while God's law is exact, there is also the mercy of God, the loving wisdom which softens the karma the soul makes for itself, and uses it to bring ultimate blessing to the soul.

'We assure you that the Great White Spirit is a God of infinite love and tenderness. And every child of God is ordained to go through experiences on earth which will bring it into that happiness and peace for which it longs.'

Trust enables you to 'let go and let God'. Trust yourself as a child of God—loved, loveable and lovely. No matter what has happened in your life, nothing can destroy that love of the Father–Mother for you. As you enter meditation with this thought you may relax; even the cells of the body can begin to relax their tension—their fight for life—and come back to harmony. Let God do the work for you.

Meditation: RECEIVING THE DIVINE ESSENCE

WE ASK you not to think about any physical disability you may have, not to concentrate upon it. Just forget it for a while. Always do this when you are receiving spiritual healing. Concentrate only upon the Great White Light, the spiritual Sun, the Sun that is the great Light, the spiritual Sun behind the physical sun. This is the life of each one, and this Light which is flowing to you from the Sun is going to right all inharmony in your body. It is going to restore balance to your body. You can breathe in this healing power.

We repeat: do not cling to your disabilities, but look into the heart of God, the heart of the Sun, and know that God is giving you His–Her healing Spirit.

If your vision can be raised to the spiritual level of life, you may see in a healing temple in the spirit spheres a number of white-robed brethren, and it is as if they carry with them 'bowls' containing healing essence. They sprinkle this essence upon those who are sick and weary, and if you open yourself to this life of the spirit you too may absorb this divine essence. It will purify your body and soul, it will cleanse it from all poison, because harmony and peace and love are great purifiers. They cleanse the whole being. And as the soul is being cleansed the body is cleansed also. Then this essence is absorbed into your heart, and the heart—being the centre or the Sun of your little individual solar system—controls all the other chakras or centres of light in your body.

When there is sickness, the origin of the disease can usually be traced to your chakras. The disharmony that comes into these chakras is created ignorantly, innocently through conflict or confusion of thought, through being out of tune with the Source of life. Weariness, mental conflict, soul-inharmony, fret or unhappiness—all these things cause a blockage in the chakras. Forget your physical ailments and concentrate on the invisible healers.

Try to imagine that you are in this temple of healing in the spiritual realms, and as you wait peacefully and surrender yourself within this healing temple, you are being purified and cleansed. The healing brotherhood is sprinkling upon you this divine essence, which is going into your heart. From your heart it is travelling all round your body in perfect order, revivifying and purifying the chakras.

8.
Look for Beauty on Earth and in Heavenly Contact

DEAR ONE, look for beauty in your everyday life. Do not take things for granted. Seek for beauty in the flowers, in the sunlight, in the dewdrop. If you can, go out in the early morning when the dew is still wet upon the grass; while it is bejewelling the gossamer cobwebs on the grass and bush. Gaze on the beauty and intricacy of the construction of the little webs and feel stirring within you an awareness of your brotherhood, your kinship with that beautiful thing.

All brethren of the Great White Lodge are aware of their relationship to all forms of life. An initiate can identify him or herself with the tiniest insect, with the flowers, the trees, the sunlight and gentle rain. This is the way all have to pass if they would enter the temple. 'Little flower, who made thee?' sang your poet*; 'If I could understand thy life, I should understand God and the universe'. And you can understand: not with your mind, but through identifying yourself with the light and with the lifestreams; by becoming at one with all life.

You can learn to step outside your personality or yourself as a limited and confining thing. You can learn to get away from yourself, from the limitations of your physical brain, and to slip away on the wings of imagery. You will find yourself free, and then—in this land of meditation, which is the real land of light—you will see behind the scenes of physical and material life, and in doing so learn the true meaning of brotherhood. You will know then that you cannot

*This is a paraphrase of Tennyson's poem, 'Flower in the crannied wall'.

serve with all your heart and all your soul and all your mind, without growing in Christlikeness. You will know that you cannot separate yourself from the great ocean of life; that you cannot hurt your brother or sister, whether he or she is of the human, animal or even vegetable kingdom, without feeling that hurt yourself.

And so we come back again to the simple teaching of our Lord and Master, Jesus Christ, the Sun and the Light: *Love one another....* *Little children, love one another....*

'You can learn to step outside your personality, or yourself as a limited and confining thing. You can learn to get away from yourself, from the limitations of your physical brain, and to slip away on the wings of imagery.'

Beauty is one of the pathways to the heaven world. Simply beholding or imagining a beautiful thing, or lovely scene, can lift the consciousness far beyond the earth. It is not simply for sensation that White Eagle describes the beauty of the heaven world, but because beauty is truly creative and regenerative. Although he here describes a certain kind of beautiful scene, if another beautiful place unfolds before you as you go into your meditation, go with it. As White Eagle says, this is *your* true home in spirit, and it can be different for each one of us. The healing Star will be there, at the heart of that which touches you deeply.

Meditation: OUR TRUE HOME

WE ARE going to take you now into a world of infinite love and harmony—your true home—a spirit world of infinite light and beauty. All around you are gardens of perfection, flower-filled; vast parklands with lakes filled with lotus blooms. We show you the flowing rivers of clear water, the banks of wild flowers, and the spring trees filled with blossom.

In the distance, there are mountains, peaks of gold, but

on the plain in the heart of these mountains is a white temple. Imagine you are moving towards it, gliding without effort to this holy, beautiful, spiritual temple of healing.

We are in a vast temple of perfect proportions. High above our heads we see an immense Star pulsating with light and colour. Beneath this Star, arranged in perfect symmetry, are resting-places: low couches, all different in colour, colours that you know and many that you do not know. The patients are brought in to rest beneath this immense Star of power and life, and the spirit and soul of the healer is the instrument to make the contact between that centre of healing and the patient.

In the silence, in this healing temple there appears the form of the Master Jesus, illumined, transfigured by the love of the Lord Christ. He says, looking up into this Star of immense dimensions: 'This is the symbol of my cosmic body. This is the bread, the life: receive it'. And he holds the cup, shaped like a heart. 'My heart of love. This is the wine. Take it. Receive the bread and the wine, my body and my spirit which are given to you. Reject not the Father's gifts, nor the gifts of my Mother. These gifts will make you whole. Receive the rays from on high and be healed in mind and body.'

Heavenly peace blesses you … peace divine … love divine. Amen.

9.
The Healing Breath

ALL PEOPLE, consciously or unconsciously, are seeking the holy breath. We wonder how many on earth realize its power, which is that of life, of wisdom and of love? May you all search for this holy breath. You will find it both in your outer life and in your inner temple.

There is much to learn about the art of breathing, which can control your life, your unfoldment and your health on the physical, mental and spiritual planes. If you will at this moment relax your mind and body, and quietly and slowly breathe deeply; and as you breathe in try to imagine that you are breathing in light and life; that you are not only inhaling air, *you are filling every particle of your being with God's breath.* As you do this you will naturally be freed from earthly problems because you will forget your body and for a fleeting moment be released. Try it. For when you thus breathe correctly, you will always find relief from the bondage of cares and limitations.

If you will follow exactly a simple practice, we are going to suggest you will find only good will result. But don't strain in any way. All breathing exercise should be harmonious and without discomfort; it should bring a sense of wellbeing:

Each morning on rising, stand, if possible, before an open window. Relax your body and breathe slowly, quietly, harmoniously, first exhaling till the lungs are completely empty, then gradually drawing the breath deeper until you are filling the lower part of the lungs and expanding the ribs as you breathe. Then exhale again, until once more the lungs are completely empty. As you inhale each breath, aspire to God; feel that God is entering into you. As you exhale, bless all life. By this inbreathing you are drawing spiritual light into your heart centre. It is like bringing spiritual sunlight and refreshment to the seed-atom resting in your heart.

'Imagine that you are breathing in light and life; that you are not only inhaling air, *you are filling every particle of your being with God's breath*. As you do this you will naturally be freed from earthly problems because you will forget your body and for a fleeting moment be released.'

The breath links the nervous system with the etheric body. Through conscious God-breathing, you strengthen your nervous system and the link to your higher self. As you begin this meditation, follow the instructions for breathing practice that White Eagle gave in the preceding contemplative passage. As you focus on the centre of light within your being, at the heart centre, imagine that light growing outwards in all directions as you breathe in. As you breathe out, let your consciousness flow out too.

Meditation: THE RADIANT LIGHT

WE WANT to take you to a place in the world of spirit. Forget your body and your lower mind. Concentrate on the centre of light within your being, and visualize a vast arena with seats or steps rising in tiers from the centre to an unimaginable height, even beyond your capacity to see....

It is like an immense sun or circle of radiant light ... most delicate, glowing with the soft radiance of the spiritual heart of life—in all you see.

As you gaze you will see that all those seats, from the base right up to beyond your vision, are filled by the vast company of white-clothed brethren. You will see that among this great gathering there is sense of expectancy. You will hear music ... the harmony of the spheres.

Now, see coming down into your vision the form of the simple, loving Master, the embodiment of the Cosmic Christ. Can you feel and respond to his blessing? Do you see the beauty of his face, the simplicity and nobility of his bearing, the wisdom and love that shines from him? Do you feel his love drawing you towards him, giving you peace, reassurance, strength? What does the outer world, where the children of life play, matter?—for here, in this amphitheatre, there is infinite power and love. It is the centre of divine will.

Oh, do you feel the enfoldment of his love? In this you

can consciously live, and from this centre you go forth to serve your brother, your sister and all life. He, the gentle Master, knows. He will give you wisdom to act rightly.

Hold this vision quietly and steadily for thirty seconds if you can and you will receive … the blessing….

Go back to your work on earth. And remember the holy breath, that is the secret.

10.
Using the Senses

IT IS VERY important that you understand the value of form, because it is through form that the spirit manifests. Not only is there physical form, there is the form of beauty in nature. Through beauty in nature you glimpse the divine spirit—this radiance, this love. Through the grandness of nature you glimpse the power of that spirit, and through the harmony of music, which is another form on the earth or in the heavens, you also see spirit. It is a form, a sound-form through which the Creator manifests. Form, the form of the healing temple, of the angels and the action of the angels, of music and of beauty in nature, is a medium through which the Great Spirit always works.

As you wander in the woods, in a temple or gardens, or as you inhale the perfume of the rose, through that perfume you make contact with your Creator, with God. And when you taste pure food, pure and beautiful fruits, when you taste the crystal water of the spring which falls from the hillside, you are tasting divine form in the water of the Creator, God.

Through all your senses of vision, of taste, of hearing, of inhaling the air and perfume, and of touching beauty, you are using all your senses to make contact with the divine Creator, with God, your Father–Mother. You cannot separate Father–Mother, for together they produce form, They produce Life.

In your healing work you are learning to call upon the angels of healing. You try to imagine their form. Many of you are able to see these bearers of the White Light, and the rays of the Christ Light, as they direct them under the instructions of the leader of the group.

They direct them to the patient, and you are able to see the patients being carried in the healing temple. Your thought creates form.

'It is very important that all of you understand the value of form, because it is through form that the spirit manifests…. Through all your senses of vision, of taste, of hearing, of inhaling the air and perfume, and of touching beauty, you make contact with the divine Creator.'

Each sense has a spiritual counterpart. We learn to develop these etheric senses in meditation. We also use our imagination to create form. It is as real, at the inner level, as that which you see and touch on earth. If you are feeling bereft, if you feel you have lost something precious to you, or if your heart feels barren, then this meditation will help you to feel the continuity of life. Offer your distress to God at the beginning of the meditation, like the empty grail cup, and then watch and feel it being filled.

Meditation: OFFERING THE GRAIL CUP OF THE HEART

NOW WE want to draw a picture: will you in your soul body kneel before the blazing golden altar in the spirit world? Upon that altar is the Holy Grail, burning so brightly, and the rays of light are streaming down into the Grail Cup. He who is the Great Healer is waiting for you, for your co-operation. He says that each one must bring to him his or her own grail cup, which really means the cup of his or her heart.

Now, using your power of imagery, create in form the grail cup, and offer it to the Great Healer, who will fill it according to its capacity. 'It is filled with the wine of life, my child, the wine of life, the Divine Essence. Now raise it to your lips and drink, for it is my life, my love, which I am giving you.' You, on earth, must create the form, the vessel. This may be with your soul substance or with physical substance, but you must create the form. And the Father–Mother in heaven uses that form to reach your heart—the grail cup.

The contents of that grail cup are both bread and wine. Underneath are the everlasting arms, for our heavenly Father–Mother will not leave you comfortless, will not leave you alone to loneliness, but will ever sustain you, and bring out of the barren land the glorious rose of heaven. And your wilderness, your desert, shall blossom with roses.

Your spirit will rejoice, my child. It will rejoice, for you will know that in God there is no separation. There is no death, but only ever-unfolding life and service, and joy in service. Be not weary, my child, but keep on within your capacity. Strive to live harmoniously, quietly, trustingly—live each hour at a time in the consciousness of the beloved, the beloved Healer.

And before we leave you we are going to take you into the garden—shall we call it the Garden of Reunion?—where the desert once was—the desert which is now blooming with roses.

Come into the Garden of Reunion, and meet your nearest and dearest, your loved one in spirit. She is there … he is there. And in this heavenly place there is this reunion of spirit with spirit, no longer hungry for love, but finding fulfilment, the perfect fulfilment of love….

May the peace of the Great White Spirit fill your hearts and minds and direct and control your life. Peace, peace, peace be with you.

11.
The Self that Knows no Fear

MAYBE YOU are sick in your body; you are weary. But there is a life within you which is going to triumph, and it knows—your inner self knows—that there is a better life for you. It knows there is a higher life and that through your freewill and your own effort you can reach out towards it above the pull of the earth. But also through the heart of others, through their sorrow and sickness and perplexity, you can find a kinship with the same source of life as theirs.

The life on earth is a valuable experience to the soul of a man or woman, and most people think that death is the greatest enemy and is to be feared. We would say to you that death is an angel that receives the newly born spirit. Fear is the enemy that robs a man and woman of all peace and happiness.

When you love God, you resign yourself into God's keeping. God is love, and through love you find God. As soon as you love you will be in direct contact with the Great Spirit and there will be no fear anywhere in you, and no darkness.

This contact is comparatively easy to achieve, this at-one-ment and this realization of the Presence, but it does not generally last: that is the snag. It very quickly fades away and the mortal mind is possessed again by the material state of life. And so this is why we say, constantly give yourselves the opportunity to make this contact with the unseen life. Seek—through prayer and meditation—knowledge of eternal life, beautiful, joyous life. Seek to tune in, to adjust yourselves to that great life—the life which is *your* life. For you have lived through countless ages—some happy lives, some the reverse—but you have been learning all the time, and the light of divinity within you is growing.

'There is a life within you which is going to triumph and it knows—your inner self knows—that there is a better life for you.'

God is both Father and Mother, and we are the children of divine parents. To keep confident in that knowledge, and in our continued existence, is one of the challenges of the spiritual path, for that faith is tested a great deal by much that we see and hear. Regular times of communion, whether in meditation or in nature, help us to reconnect with the source of our being and restore us. In this meditation, begin by imagining yourself being nurtured in the way you most need. Let all your senses be open to feel the presence of those who would help you.

Meditation:
THE GREAT MOTHER

CLOSE YOUR physical eyes and your physical senses and attune your being to the spirit Lodge—that is, the place of meeting in the world of spirit, the spirit temple. Leave aside, or behind you, the earth plane, remembering that you are spirit. While still in your physical body you have to realize that you are spirit, and that there is a higher world, a more beautiful state of life which is your true home. You have to realize that you have left that true home to come into earth conditions just as a child goes to school. But a child is not always at school; it sometimes goes home and we want you to come home for a few short minutes.

Come up, dear one, come up into our world of spirit. Open your inner vision. Free the spiritual creative power. Follow our description of the temple in which you are now assembled, the temple of healing, built by your creative power, the power of your spirit. It is a temple not built by hands but by your spirit. It is very fair indeed, being constructed of a spiritual or soul substance. The great pillars are built of light and the colours of the spectrum can be seen pulsating in the substance of which the temple is built.

See the patients all assembled round the altar, which is in the very centre of the temple … the altar of pure white substance. The patients and healers, angelic healers as well as human forms, are ready, waiting for the coming of the Holy Spirit. She comes—as the Divine Mother. All-loving Mother comes, She who has understanding of your needs and of the weariness of the flesh; the Great Mother comes.

And now another Being appears in a great light—the Christ—and the Great White Spirit pours down upon you the golden rays from heaven…. Your cup, the grail cup that is your heart, is being filled, filled with the power of the spirit. The Holy Grail is the mystical cup that holds the divine essence of Christ's love.

Perhaps you will see the great angel of the sun with wings outstretched, guarding the sacred Holy Grail; and perhaps you will see the form of the gentle Christ standing with the grail cup before him. And he will smile into your eyes and will raise the cup to your lips … and you will drink deeply. This golden liquid will flow all through your being, pulsating through every atom, the physical, mental and spiritual atoms of which you are composed.

Be filled…. Filled with this balm…. We surrender to Thee, O Great Father–Mother God.

12. True Healing

TRUE HEALING takes place on the spiritual plane, and healing power comes from the Christ sphere. According to the purity of the healer, it pours through his subtler vehicles and flows from her hands. It streams indeed from the healer's whole aura. Healing depends not so much on the laying-on of hands, but on a clear and full contact with Christ. The essence of Christ can then pour forth from the whole aura and can be intensified in its actions by the healer's mental control. This is the true healing.

Spiritual healing is brought about by the power of spiritual aspiration. When the thoughts are truly aspiring, then the light of Christ, the rays of Christ, fall into the heart. As soon as the rays of Christ are felt in the physical body, then having great power they can reverse the order of things. Where the physical body is dark, light takes possession, dominating the body and controlling the physical atoms. This is how miracles are performed. When we say that thought has the power to do this, we of course mean divine thought, the thought which rises from a pure and aspiring heart. The power which comes when the heart is set upon God can reverse negative to positive, darkness to light; the inflowing of the light will produce perfect health because it will produce harmony.

'As soon as the rays of Christ are felt in the physical body, having great power they can reverse the order of things. Where the physical body is dark, light takes possession, dominating the body and controlling the physical atoms. This is how miracles are performed.'

In a healing meditation, you are focusing on those rays of Christ, opening a channel for them to flow from the higher etheric, through the lower, into the physical body. Love will enable this to happen. So, as you begin your meditation, think of an earthly love you have: not necessarily of a person, but maybe of something in the natural world. Bring into your consciousness the feeling of loving … and then imagine that love magnified by your inner spirit—beyond emotionalism and desire—into something so powerful it can transform your life.

Meditation: SPIRITUAL SUBSTANCE

NOW BELOVED one, be silent…. Enter the inner planes, the sanctuary of the heart of love…. You are encompassed by the white-robed brethren there.

There is one here in your midst—a gentle brother—one who understands all your needs. His body is shining with this spiritual light, and he brings to you the bread and the communion cup. In the silence let us all partake of this golden liquid, the spiritual life-force which he is pouring out on to the earth, and receive into our hearts the healing power of the golden spiritual life.

Your heart centre is opening in sweet simplicity and in love, and in that state you are able to receive the outflow of golden light from the heart of the Lord Jesus Christ. As you receive this golden ray, your heart centre is stimulated and you are able to partake of the bread of life.

The bread of life is the divine spirit within you which is stimulated, which becomes alive, which becomes a power in you and in your life. This is the spiritual substance of the Cosmic Christ. This is why it is called the body of Christ. It is the cosmic substance that is the body of Christ, and this cosmic substance which you are receiving into yourself causes that divine life within you to become stronger, causes it to grow. You are satisfied, but you need constant replenishment, constant reception of that golden ray to stimulate the Christ within you, and this is the meaning of the bread. When you are offered the bread, use your inner awareness and realize that this Christ life within you is being fed. The Lord Jesus Christ offers you the bread of life. Take; eat; absorb the substance of His cosmic body....

Then he gathers wine in the chalice. He gathers it from the great heart of Christ. It is like drops of his life's blood, spiritual not physical blood, which fall into that cup, and it is offered to you to sip. You do this consciously knowing that it is as real to you as a material cup. It is there before you; you take and you sip, and you are stimulated by the divine fire that floods your being. 'My life shared with you. My life-force. It flows from my heart. It is my love and it is this love that I give to you. Take; drink. It is my strength, my life; become part of my life. Be healed in body and soul, and come up into the sun, into the eternal life of my Father–Mother in heaven.' You receive it into yourself and you become a little more conscious of your union with Christ....

'Do this constantly in remembrance of the life of the Son of God, the Son which is the light and the life, the Son which is in you. *My peace I leave with you*....

'Amen.'

13.
The Note of Love

TO OUR BELOVED servers in healing we should like to say this. Always endeavour, when you are called to the healing work, to strike a chord or a note. We suggest to you that to strike this note you bring into action your pure spirit, the spirit of Christ love. Lay aside all troubles, thoughts of the earth. Seek control of your emotion, and your nervous reactions. Seek the stillness and know that I AM GOD—that still small voice, the voice of the Spirit ... which sounds. The *sound of it*, reverberating through the whole of life.

This sound not only touches the human life, it touches all life throughout your universe. In the garden, the flowers are touched by the vibration which flows or sounds from your heart, from the heart of love. The animal kingdom will respond not merely to the sound of the human voice, but to the sound within the human heart.

We are saying these things to you because your healing is something more than laying-on of hands, something more than words which you repeat in your absent healing service. Healing goes on all the time, because the healing power is not merely the light which flows through your hands from the Spirit sphere of life. It is the vibration, the note which you sound from your heart, which is like a harp—God's harp.

This note which you are plucking not only affects you, and those human beings with whom you come into contact daily. We mean not only letters you write, and the conversation you have, either mouth-to-ear, or in a telephone message. By your vibration you heal; the vibration which you allow to sound in your soul, in your heart. All this work goes on unconsciously, you are quite unconscious that it is that simple, pure love which you are sending forth.

'Seek the stillness and know that I AM GOD—that still small voice the voice of the Spirit ... which sounds. The *sound of it*, reverberating through the whole of life.'

You may like to begin your meditation either by listening to voices chanting, or singing something uplifting, or by chanting a mantra yourself if you are familiar with doing this. Chanting the great *Aum*—the word of God, the creative word of life—White Eagle says, can actually clear the thought-atmosphere around and through your aura. If your mind is busy or you have been distracted by a lot of mental influences, this is a way to bring peace into your mental aura in preparation for finding the stillness. It does not have to be loud, but make sure you will not be disturbed—you can even imagine chanting if need be, because most important is that you chant with awareness of what you are calling forth....

Meditation: THE STILLNESS OF THE HEART

BRETHREN, in the deep stillness of the heart, when the mind is at peace, when the cares of the world are released, in that deep stillness of the heart you will find God. God will speak to you in the silence and the stillness of the heart….

It is in this stillness, this total stillness, when truly the heart is open to the great love of God, that the true healing is accomplished. When the heart is still and filled with love, you become a channel, an instrument…. No effort is required, just the stillness of love—and then you become a channel for the light of the Great Healer to flow to humanity.

Try to become ever more still in your heart, and totally attune to the Star, the perfect balance of the Star. Become *as* the Star, a radiant light, so that there is no limit to the radiation of the light you can send forth.

Let go all that is a barrier, all that binds you to fear, to lack of confidence, to the problems of the earth. Feel that they can all be resolved in this perfect love of God. All will be solved from the stillness of the heart, as you let go and offer your heart and your cares to God.

In this Great Light you will be healed, cleansed, strengthened, and perfected….

14.
No Death

EVERY SOUL that is due to leave the physical body is known already on our side of life. Preparation is made; angels are waiting to receive the soul, and it is carried away in a most gentle and beautiful way, and settled in its new surroundings.

When you think about leaving the physical body, you think that that is the end. But no, you just lose consciousness for a time—sometimes only a very brief time—and then you awaken to a beautiful world of your own. When you come into the spirit world, whether it is in meditation, or after you leave your physical body, one of the first things that you will feel is the love of God. Usually the soul wakens to the beauties of nature. It may find itself lying on a green bank that is beautifully covered in turf, like a velvet carpet, with little spring flowers. Sometimes the soul awakens in a room, lying on a blue couch, with windows open to the garden, where it can look out on the mass of flowers there.

We have told you this for a special reason, for those of you who may be sad at the separation from loved ones by death just now. We want you to bear this in mind: that death is a beautiful transition. It is angels coming to release the bolts of the imprisoned soul—to release the bolts of the prison door and let the soul free.* And the angels take that unconscious soul away from earthly conditions into the purity and peace of a lovely new world. So do not be sad for them. Remember that all beings are cared for by a greater love than anyone on earth could possibly understand. All is well, for God is love.

*See the quotation from James Russell Lowell on p. 156.

'We want you to bear this in mind: that death is a beautiful transition.'

One of the ways to prepare for the transition of death is to practise, in meditation, surrendering consciously to the beauty and peace of the inner world: the world to which we will all return when our time comes. For some people that act of surrender brings fear, but in moving consciously into this space we begin, gradually, to feel and see the reality of the spiritual life while we are on earth. In the end this brings a deep and abiding confidence that death is indeed a 'beautiful transition'. Whatever your fear at this moment, move into it as you close your eyes, as if you were entering a tunnel, but see immediately as you do so, the pure Light at the end.

Meditation: THE CLEANSING OF THE SOUL

WHATEVER the aches or pains or sufferings of your body, we bring you the message which we hope will lift you up and help you to make the contact with that pure Light.

We want you to come with us in your thoughts, in your souls, to the higher realms of life. There we find ourselves in a temple of beauty and simplicity. There are twelve pillars to this temple and a pure white floor. It appears to be stone, but it is warm, much warmer than a cold stone floor. There are people seated in lotus posture on this floor. Can you get the picture? Look at their faces and see the light radiating from them. See the peace exuding from them. Feel it: the purity, perfection, holiness (which means healthfulness). Rest, my children, in this atmosphere, in the higher realms!

Now the brethren who are Masters rise. They take you, one by one, by the hand. They lead you down three steps from the floor of the temple into a garden. Do you see the atmosphere pulsating with light and power? Do you see the exquisite layout of this garden, the green lawns and the flowerbeds across which you are being led, towards an oblong healing pool of cleansing water? Water is the great cleanser of the aura and of the soul body.

See the shining forms of angelic healers as they stand there waiting for you. Now the healing guides are waiting to take you through the cleansing ceremony. Do you remember the baptism in the river Jordan? This has the same esoteric meaning. All healing, all cleansing, all purification must take place in the individual soul. The outer form has an inner spiritual significance and a great power. If you can give yourselves to this ceremony you will undoubtedly feel the effects in your physical body.

You are led to the angels at the pool, and the water is first sprinkled on your head, because the mind of earth needs cleansing, purifying. Then you are taken down the three steps into the pool and you are covered in water up to your neck. You are taken slowly through the water. You are helped out at the other side, and in the distance you will see a golden light. It is raised on a small hilltop. You are being led towards it. The air is growing purer, more invigorating, and you feel that you have lost a heavy burden. You have surrendered in love to the Golden One.

You feel the enfoldment, the power, the strength. You are being recreated by His spirit. His helpers are with you, helping you to move nearer and nearer to that golden Light. And the golden light has changed, and in its place is the form of the shepherd holding the crook: *I AM the good shepherd, and know my sheep*. He draws you close to his heart.

'Lead me, Lord', you pray; 'lead me'. He points upward to the Father–Mother God. This is the secret, he says. Relax, children of earth, in his love—that is all. Feel the healing flowing through you. If you will receive it you will never lack: never, never. 'Peace, dear one, peace be unto you.' And in our midst flutters the white dove, the heavenly symbol of the Holy Presence. Amen.

15. Draw Closer to God

LET US BE still in body and mind and seek the place of silence where the voice of God can be heard. This is the way, the truth. So much activity abounds in the physical world, the astral world and the mental world that the true place of happiness is scarcely entered.

On one occasion, when we were trying to describe the radiance of a master soul, we placed before our listeners a mental picture of a flashing jewel, in the centre of which was to be seen the perfect form of the Son of God, the Christ form. We explained that every human being contains within itself the power to grow into that perfect jewel. But how to get started—how to receive the inspiration and illumination which appears to be necessary before the soul can see its goal clearly? That is your problem.

The first essential is to draw each day into closer communion with God. So few understand this great blessing of communion with the Infinite Spirit. The soul who would set forth and progress on the journey towards the supreme goal must maintain conscious companionship with God. This will not come about through prayers that are no more than words, but only through simple, trusting communion with the Great Spirit.

The Infinite Spirit is everywhere; people live and move and have their being within the arms of the Infinite. You live in God, and God is continually present in you. God is omnipresent, omniscient, omnipotent. These will seem only words to you but it is for you to discover for yourselves their living reality.

How true is the saying, 'Underneath are the everlasting arms'! The reality of infinite, all-enfolding love—this is essential for the soul to realize.

'So much activity abounds in the physical world, the astral world and the mental world that the true place of happiness is scarcely entered…. The reality of infinite, all-enfolding love—this is essential for the soul to realize.'

The next meditation begins in the golden light—the colour of the sun, of strength, warmth and creative power. The golden light is the beacon on the top of the mountain that draws your consciousness to higher realms. By ascending the mountain you will go on to find the blue lake of healing. Blue is the colour associated with peace and devotion. When you reach this point, feel yourself surrounded by a blue of the most heavenly shade and depth you can imagine. Love for and yearning for God can help this colour to become more real for you.

Meditation:
THE BLUE POOL OF HEALING

DEAR ONE, we would draw you up to the top of the golden mountain, to the highest pinnacle of spiritual consciousness of which you are capable. There, through your imagination—think of it as your soul vision—you may see the Master with arms outstretched, calling you to come up to him and be comforted and enfolded in his love.

Open your heart that it may be a receptacle to these golden rays of creative power and life and health. He draws aside the veil of materiality beyond which you will see the altar in the golden temple of the Son of God. There you will see him in this heavenly life in all its purity and holiness. As you come closer to the altar, keep your vision above the earth—upon the face of the beloved Christ.

He calls upon God to bless the bread, which he breaks into many pieces before he distributes them to each soul in his presence. Take, eat the bread of heaven. Absorb the food of your soul, and give forth all your love and compassion to your brethren of all the kingdoms of earth.

And the Master raises the cup of wine. He calls down once again the blessing of his Father upon this wine, the essence of his love for you. Drink, drink from the cup, that your heart may be full of love, for love is the fulfilling of the law. Through love you are made whole.

Now your soul is taken through the healing and

cleansing waters. Use your powers of heavenly imagery and see the blue waters—the healing waters. Feel yourselves being guided through this cleansing process. This is what the body and soul of a person on earth needs more than physical food. He or she needs this washing, this cleansing of the etheric body. Feel yourself being immersed in the blue pool of healing, and all the dark fearful atoms fall away from you. Look up into the tender smile of the Master Jesus.

And his angels lead you forth into the spirit garden of perfect flowers. Peace, peace, peace be unto you. The healing of the soul is far more important than that of the body. In the calmness of your spirit try and retain the peace of this heavenly spiritual garden. Just surrender yourself to the infinite love, wisdom and power of the Divine Master. You cannot fail to breathe into yourself the Breath of God, and you will go forth to live in harmony with God's law—love.

16. Making Contact with the Light

WE ARE permitted to come to you from the world of spirit to bring you that power which will lift you up and give you both peace of mind and strength of body. But it is not enough that we bring you this power: you, on your part, must strive to realize your true plane of life.

You believe in an invisible life and an invisible power that will heal you of sickness and confusion of mind and spirit, and of aches and pains and inharmonies in your physical body, but this power needs to find a point of entry into you. You have to prepare your mind, your soul and your body for the inflow of this divine healing.

Try to realize that you are not the physical body, any more than you are the clothes you wear. Your body is like your form of dress, and when the great transition comes to you, you will lay it aside as you lay aside your material clothing. But your true self, your invisible self, lies deep within you, covered up not only by the coat of skin, but by the other emanations or bodies such as the mental body, the emotional body and the astral body. Think of peeling off these various bodies, or of opening your coats one by one. There, deep within your heart centre, beneath these many layers, is the holy of holies, the light....

When you turn within to this innermost centre, this pure spirit, and dwell with this spirit, which is all love, you are opening the way for the inflow of the Christ healing.

Once you can make contact with the light, which is at the apex of the triangle of your being, you will lose hesitancy. Step right forward on the path and you will find that feet and legs, knees, the parts of you which should walk firmly, boldly, will become healed. If you consider your body as an engine, there is no reason why you should not refuel every organ of it with a fresh supply of the pure oil of life. Do this each day—take in your supply of fuel. It can be done in a flash—this is not impossible. You can be healed by steady persistent realization of this divine light. Your body is the temple of God, and as such it must be preserved.

'Your true self, your invisible self, lies deep within you, covered up not only by the coat of skin, but by the other emanations or bodies such as the mental body, the emotional body and the astral body. Think of peeling off these various bodies, or of opening your coats one by one; and there, deep within your heart centre, beneath these many layers, is the holy of holies, the light.'

One way of relaxing before meditation is to imagine shedding heavy clothing layer by layer, as your face, neck, shoulders, belly and thighs let go. You can do this with each outbreath, while with each inbreath you feel the inner, spiritual self arising from within and expanding in the light of the sun.

Meditation: A CRYSTAL TEMPLE

WE LEAD you into a temple of healing, a white temple. All the fabric of the temple is pure white and yet it contains all the rays of the Christ light. We are in the centre of a large circle of angelic beings. Our temple is open on all sides to nature, to a sunlit garden. Flowers are there, fountains, running brooks. Centre your thoughts upon these....

Above our heads in this temple is a jewel, a star, cut in a very special way so that the rays from the sun, which penetrate it, shine through in different colours. The pure ray from the sun is split up into many different colours, and according to your need your spirit will select one or more of these rays.

Do not think of your symptoms, but just surrender your whole being to the rays of the spiritual Sun. That spiritual Sun is the heart of the great being, Christ, the Lord of earth's humanity....

He brings to you the bread of life, the cosmic body of the Sun. Take, absorb this bread. It will feed you, nourish you, sustain you....

He brings you the cup of golden liquid—the wine, the divine life essence. Drink.... I AM the way to life.

I AM divine peace ... divine peace ... divine peace.

I AM divine love ... divine love ... divine love.

I AM within your heart.

17.
Out of Limitation and Imprison- ment

WE DO NOT advise you to strain after anything, but we do guide you sincerely and gently to seek the vision of a higher life. The physical cares weigh heavily upon all who are imprisoned in the body, yet we would remind you that the light of Christ is in you, in your heart. Become, as he advised you to become, as little children— simple and believing. Then the still, small voice within you will urge you to believe that God is the source of your life. God *is* the life; resign yourself to God, remembering that God is ever-creative; the mind of God, Divine Intelligence, is forever creating and recreating. As soon as you can come into communion with that power you are being recreated.

Are you troubled about your affairs? Then keep very calm, very still, and say to God: 'Thou art all wisdom. Thou art all love. Thy will is being done'. Then you yourself must try not to doubt that the best thing *is* happening and that out of the present limitation and imprisonment you *will* be released. The angel of the Lord will visit you and will release your chains and lead you forth into freedom and happiness.

As you yourself have faith in God's love, so will the light in you grow and expand. *Knock and the door of heaven will be opened unto you.* Ask now in the silence, and you shall receive.

Lo, I am with you always. A holy peace rests upon you.

'Ask now in the silence, and you shall receive.
'Lo, I am with you always. A holy peace rests upon you.'

To begin your meditation, imagine that although your eyes are
closed, you are looking down towards the centre of your chest, and
inwards in consciousness, towards your heart chakra. Imagine that
you can look into another dimension where a tiny point of light, like
a distant star, shines. As you gently breathe, the light from that
star or sun grows brighter and closer, and a great feeling of stillness
enfolds you….

Meditation: THE COSMIC UNIVERSE

WE ARE aware that some of you are crying out for guidance. Do not look outside for this help, but within. Look to the pure spiritual source of love and strength.

You have nothing to fear. You are not alone. Open wide the gates, and the comfort and light will flow into your heart, into your physical body and material life. As the power of the Holy Spirit poured down on the disciples at Whitsuntide, as they waited, so the power pours down on you.

Enter into the silence for a while and open your vision and see the glory of the company of shining souls. Watch the sun rising in the east and all these souls silently waiting. As the sun slowly rises over the horizon, there appears in the heart of the sun the Christ—the source of creation. With this vision there come countless stars and planets; we are looking right into the cosmos. All are one in this vast panorama of pulsating life.

Now we see the reflected light of the sun on other worlds and on our moon. We want you to become aware in your souls of this cosmic universe. Breathe and live in the consciousness of this infinite and eternal cosmic life.

There stands forth from the company the beloved Master, Jesus. From him you may absorb into your heart this light, this love, this spiritual fragrance. Breathe and absorb the blessing of the Holy Spirit. The symbol of the white bird descends....

18.
Miracles

EVENTUALLY, you will see that the answer to every human problem lies in that simple heart-love which is harmony, which is God. God makes all crooked places straight. Therefore withdraw, withdraw yourself from whatever human problem is yours at this very moment. Drop it, surrender it—in other words, give it up to the divine spirit. Have confidence in the source of your being, the Great Light. Your problem will then no longer trouble you. You will know within that God will answer. All will be well. This is a spiritual state to which the soul has to attain, and when the soul has attained the level of surrender to God, the power will work.

When we say 'surrender', it does not mean entering into a state of apathy. Surrender means a strong certainty in the soul that all is working for good. It requires effort on your part. It requires control of the emotions, a stillness of the mind, a holiness or healthfulness. We would explain: holiness means healthfulness and healthfulness means holiness, a state of body and mind which has to be striven for, worked for, in order that surrender may be achieved. Then the divine life takes possession and works miracles.

Miracles are things the ordinary mind cannot comprehend. But miracles are the natural outworking of divine law over the physical state. The divine law controls and manipulates matter, but only because the limited human self stands on the side. Then those who do not comprehend divine law say, 'How extraordinary, a miracle has happened!' But miracles happen first in the soul.

The miracles described in the Bible are soul-experiences as well as physical manifestations. Divine miracles within the soul become miracles in the physical state. That is how miracles happen through matter.

'Miracles are things which the ordinary mind cannot comprehend. But miracles are the natural outworking of divine law over the physical state.'

Meditation can be a very healing experience. Simply being still and focusing on something other than worldly concerns can bring a sense of relief and relaxation to the cells of the body as well as the mind. Before entering meditation, focus on something you think of as lovely, something beautiful, and this will begin the process of release. It may only be a memory you have of a beautiful place, or it could be some object around you that you find pleasing. Doing this changes your emotional state and raises your vibrations so that the angels can draw close....

Meditation: THE HEALING ANGELS

PUT ASIDE all the worldly thoughts which crowd the earthly mind, and open wide the door of your soul to the up-rush of the eternal and the divine spirit within....

Be still, and seek the silence of the Spirit. Here you can hold communion with the angels of healing. Open your soul, be at rest, be relaxed, feel no sense of strain or tension; the angelic ones—not only the discarnate human brethren, but the angelic brethren—can then be very real to you. Be conscious of them, and see a Light never before seen, shining within....

Look to that Light, dear one. Give your heart and soul into the keeping of that Light.... It is the Light of God that surrounds you, encompasses you, and in that light the hosts of angel beings draw close....

Be receptive to the vibrations of love and beauty that now interpenetrate the world around you: an invisible and intangible beauty of love. Reach out from the depths of your being, open wide, and in the very act of opening your mind and your heart to love you become love and are in harmony with the Infinite.

And now, my beloved, will you try to touch the great heart of love...? Its wisdom, love and power fills you. May all fears fall away, and may you be conscious of a deep peace....

19. The Comforter

HE THAT believeth on me, the works that I do shall he do also; and greater works than these shall he do....
If ye love me, keep my commandments. And I will pray the Father, and he shall give you another Comforter, that he may abide with you for ever. (St John 14 : 12, 15–16)

How wonderful and beautiful is this teaching in your Bible! *He shall give you another Comforter*, which will not depend upon any bodily manifestation of Jesus. The holy breath, the Holy Ghost, will enter your innermost being and its presence will be eternal. In a sense this is a promise to each human soul of the union of the psyche or soul with the Spirit which gives it eternal life.

What is this Holy Ghost? The Holy Ghost is the in-breathing of wisdom and of love. By the way you live, if you follow the example of Jesus, there will come to you this baptism, this in-breathing of the Holy Ghost; this is the initiation of the divine fire, the divine wisdom within. Turn to inward contemplation and meditation and the holy breath enters and is felt, indescribable in words. It is a manifestation of the divine fire, the divine magic.

The Comforter, which is the Holy Ghost, whom the Father will send in my name, he shall teach you all things, and bring all things to your remembrance, whatsoever I have said unto you.

Peace I leave with you, my peace I give unto you: not as the world giveth, give I unto you. Let not your heart be troubled, neither let it be afraid. (John 14 : 26–7)

'Let not your heart be troubled, neither let it be afraid.'

The image of walking up a mountainside, or finding oneself gazing at a golden peak, is symbolic of the raising of one's consciousness. You may find an actual image of a mountain peak is helpful as a beginning focus for your meditation. Imagine such a peak in the world of spirit, where the air is pure, but not cold or thin, and the sun does not burn, and of course, the journey there does not exhaust you because it is only a thought away! Put yourself in touch with the feeling you might have of freedom, as you leave behind the heaviness of the earth, and ascend towards the beauty and light of the spiritual consciousness....

Meditation: ABOVE ALL FEARS

LIFT YOUR heart to the hills, to the mountains, to the windswept skies, to the rain-drenched earth, to the beauty and power of nature. Worship the grandeur and glory of our Creator's handiwork, and, becoming in tune with the infinite Spirit, awaken to the beauty within yourself....

Arise and walk across the valley to ascend the mountains beyond, until you stand, at last, face to face with the Christ. In the silence, on the mountaintop, with the canopy of heaven's peace spread over you, the stars of the eternal wisdom to guide you, there you meet. There God, in His–Her great love, raises you up, and the Christ child is born within your heart.

From these higher planes of consciousness you may witness, with clearness of vision, the love streaming forth upon humanity. See the wisdom guiding all life upward towards the light.

You yearn to become united in fuller consciousness with the glory of God our Father–Mother, and in this communion you learn to fold to your heart our brethren of the human and animal kingdoms. May all fear leave you, and may you know love and beauty and peace. Deep within, worship the great spirit of light, wisdom and power.

The light of the Master's countenance shines upon your path.... Allow yourself to be guided by the gentleness and the loveliness of Christ. Walk in the path of humility and quietness, knowing that all things are working together for good, for God.

Under his supreme control, and in his love and wisdom you need have no fear ... *no fear*. All is well.

20.
Negativity is Transient

NOW TRUTH is very simple. It is also profound, with a profundity beyond the reach of intellect. He or she who would find this truth within must first become simple, as a child is simple in its affection and belief, simple in its response to kindliness, in its love for life. All beauty, love and kindliness are essentially true; and it is also true that once you have yourself become simple you will begin to understand profound truths which cannot be glimpsed or grasped without this simplicity of heart.

Fear is the great enemy of any such realization of truth. You can begin to change this condition; you can refuse to believe that negative things are as real as they seem. Only by your attitude and reaction to them are they lent a sort of reality.

Train yourself to look habitually into the light of God. See Christ within your heart encompassing the world by his love. Learn not to entertain or talk about depressing things, nor become immersed in symptoms of disease or descriptions of pain and suffering, because all the while your subconscious will be listening, taking it all in, only to reproduce it in some form in your own self. Remember always that what appears threatening, painful and destructive to the outer self must by its very nature be something transient. Negative things disperse and destroy themselves simply because it is their nature to do so.

Maybe you are at the moment sick? Try to realize that this sickness is something you are steadily building up within your mind if you nourish fear of it. Refuse to accept what is being so insidiously suggested. But of course you must remember also that you cannot ride roughshod over what are called 'natural laws'. That is to say, while you are young in spiritual truth you must to a degree defer to preconceived opinions and not refuse to seek the aid of medical science if this be thought necessary. Do the wise and right things with all your problems of health or sickness in these early stages. Later, as you learn to live more calmly and placidly, you will be able to resist and rise above these problems by the power of Christ in you.

Your own part of becoming whole and healthy is to forget your symptoms and to concentrate instead on the Source of all life and light, from which alone can come peace and tranquillity of spirit. Set your heart resolutely on the things of God, the things of heaven, and all that is needed will be given to you.

'You can refuse to believe that negative things are as real as they seem. Only by your attitude and reaction to them are they lent a sort of reality.'

To think of being well is such a hard thing to do when the body clamours for attention, or the emotions are stirred by suffering. Meditation, if possible at such a time, can be the greatest help. Conscious breathing practice, whether or not it ends in meditation, will strengthen the nervous system to cope with the fear and negativity. As you begin your meditation, it may be helpful to repeat to yourself as you breathe out, 'I breathe away fear and negativity'. As you breathe in say, 'I breathe in the light. All is more perfect than it seems'.

Meditation: THE BLUE COUCH

ALL LIFE is God, and when a person can leave the entanglements of the earthly self and dwell in the consciousness of the eternal good he or she is immediately in heaven, and knows no limitation. This is the truth.

Now, dear one, leave the entanglements of your mind and your physical conditions, shut out all discordance and doubt and fear and criticism of spiritual things, and just come up, up into the world of Light.

There in that world we see the temple of healing, the temple built of the Light. Before we enter this healing temple we see in front of us a large lake or pool of blue water. It is a cleansing pool, the healing pool. Allow yourselves to be led through this healing pool and up the dazzling white path into the healing temple, and you will see the whiteness therein and the Light, as though the sun is shining right in the temple itself.

You will see the couches draped with blue spiritual material. You will see the patients being guided to these couches of healing so that they may rest and relax. There is no limit to the number of these alcoves containing the blue healing couch, and every one who desires the healing treatment allows him- or herself to be led there by the ministering angel.

Be aware of lying completely relaxed on a blue couch

with your face turned towards the Sun, conscious of warm, gentle sunlight. Breathe in this Light. It is the life of God. It is the life which will make you whole. In spirit there is neither pain nor disease, because spirit is perfect. Spirit is at one with God, is part of God. You are spirit, perfect in God.

Beloved sons and daughters of earth, look up again in this temple of Eternal Light and you will see the blazing Star, symbol of Christ, the Perfect One. And the Star takes the form of the Lord, the Christ. The Cosmic Christ takes the form of man–woman to help you to realize his love and understanding for you, for you.

He stretches forth his hand to bless the symbols of communion … the cosmic bread, the matter from which all life is created, and he calls it 'my body'. It is the substance of the body of creation. He says, 'Take and eat'—of this substance, this cosmic substance—'it is my body'. And he holds before your lips the chalice of wine and says, 'Drink, for this is my spiritual life-force, my spirit; drink, and feel it flow all through your bodies, celestial and higher mental, mental, emotional and physical'.

You are at one with all life. You are perfected in God. Peace be in your soul. Be healed and recreated in your Father–Mother God.

21.
How to Relax

THE PHYSICAL body of necessity has its limitations, until its karma releases it from them. Therefore do not neglect times of relaxation. Brother body, who is your servant, needs your love and your wisdom. Do not overtax yourself, nor overstrain in your eagerness to accomplish much work, even if the motive is good. *Love thy neighbour as thyself*—which means 'love your brother or sister the same as you love yourself, and vice versa'. It is like walking a razor-edge, but it is the right and true way.

When you relax, you are giving yourself, your body, the time it needs to be recharged, replenished. We know that the demands of life are very hard, particularly at the stage in human development you are experiencing, but do remember to relax whenever you can. By 'relax' we mean just going to God, tuning yourself into God-consciousness, and going easy; slacken off the tension in the physical body. Withdraw from the world; go into your own room, into your own inner spiritual sanctuary, and pray before the symbol of the blazing Christ Star; not only will you see that Star before you, but you will know that it is all round you, above you and beneath you.

The rays from that Star correspond to the seven colours of the spectrum on your earth—though in our world they are more than duplicated—and they will enter your body and you may breathe them in. You will say: 'How do they enter my body?' They will enter your body through your heart. They will go up right through your body to the head and down the back, right to the feet, making a circular movement. Whatever colour is most lacking in you that your physical health needs, that colour ray will be selected from the Christ Light and will penetrate just the right centre or chakra for your need. You will be cleansed and recharged.

Mentally, visually, take in those rays, and when you have been recharged the instinct within you will be to give forth. You will then be tuned-up and ready to give all the healing power that flows through you.

'We know that the demands of life are very hard, particularly at the stage in human development you are experiencing, but do remember to relax whenever you can. By 'relax' we mean just going to God, tuning yourself into God-consciousness, and going easy....'

The neck carries a great deal of tension—in more ways than one! If you can relax your neck, then much will follow. Imagine the neck is like the strings of a marionette. Put your hands, metaphorically, under the feet of the marionette and the strings go loose. Feel that sensation, particularly at the centre of the back of the neck, followed by a softening of the eyes and temples. Whenever your mind wanders during meditation, slacken the strings again. God's hands hold you up.

Meditation: THE PERFECT PLACE TO RELAX

AND NOW, dear one, we will take you in your mind—in your soul—to a place of healing above the earth. Forget that earthly mind which is denying you access to a wonderful world of spirit. 'Oh', you say, 'if only I could believe'. Just let yourself go as a little child entering a beautiful garden. There is so much to see: flowers and birds, many-coloured butterflies, masses of flowers, flowering trees and shrubs; all the beauties of a perfect garden. You may see them, and be attracted by the green lawns. You may be attracted by the little stream which runs through the garden and the green banks on either side. Throw yourselves down upon these lawns; rest—relax—let yourself go completely limp—surrender to this all-powerful spirit that is beginning to unfold in you.

Many of the diseases of the physical body are due to strain and fear and anxiety. Surrender in complete acceptance of God's love. Rest in this spirit garden, forgetting all fearful thoughts and even pain.

And now the healing angel comes to you; raises you up very gently and lovingly and guides you to the blue lake in this beautiful healing garden. The angel takes you into that blue lake until you are completely covered with that soft blue substance, a spiritual substance. Go into it right up to your neck, and you feel the weight and the heaviness of earth falling away for you. This is the lake of purification.

Now you are taken away from this blue healing water into the temple of healing, a beautiful white structure, with alcoves all round the walls at different levels; and here patients are taken to rest. Here you are healed again by the angelic healers. The aura is cleansed again and the healing power is poured into you. Above each couch is a six-pointed Star of beautiful light. The rays of this Star are pouring into you.

22. The Greatest Healer of All

ALL THE world needs healing and the great healer of all is love. So many organizations on earth seek to help in the cause of peace and progress, and all these organizations have their place, for they appeal to the varying mentality of men and women. But there is one common denominator—all souls will respond to love. It is so simple, so simple that some may get tired of hearing the words, *Love one another … or, The kingdom of heaven is within.* But this is all, it is the completeness of life—to love, to be love, to become at one with love, to become part of the whole of love.

Love is wisdom, love and wisdom are power. To love is not to have great knowledge, but to be wise. When we see true wisdom, we see love and gentleness and peace. The Master, the Great Healer, did not and could not withhold love. Do you see the implication of this? Love, which is wisdom, is the greatest power of creation; love radiates light, it heals, it comforts. Can you picture the Master of love, a powerful light, a beautiful personality, a gentle spirit whose aura reached out to touch and restore?

Those who cried out for healing, drawn by his radiance, opened themselves to love and truth. And you, who come to serve, to do something in the world which will be of use: we want you to understand that as you feel the gentleness of the Master's love in your breast, as you think of the world and all human problems with love and compassion and tenderness, so you are sending forth, either to a small or great degree, that same Christ love, to heal and to bless. As you continue to give of yourself, day by day, that you may become the bearer of that love, so the power and accompanying wisdom will grow within you.

If you contemplate and meditate upon the presence of the beautiful Christ spirit you will be filled with the spiritual perfume of that great Being. The essence of perfume of this great One will enter into your physical atoms, raising you in vibration so that all tiredness and heaviness depart. You will not know tiredness when you come to the edge of the aura of this Great One. We tell you; it is for you to experience for yourselves. You will remember the healings that took place when the crowds pressed round the beloved Master? Just coming into his aura was sufficient to revitalize the soul of the one who was to be healed. We say once again, as we have said so often before, that the one truth, the one power which the world is waiting for is the power of this pure and holy spirit, this Christ spirit. We cannot convince you with words, we can only endeavour to impart to you the essence of divine love. Come to the edge of the aura of the Christ.

'Love, which is wisdom, is the greatest power of creation; love radiates light, it heals, it comforts.... You will remember the healings that took place when the crowds pressed round the beloved Master? Just coming into his aura was sufficient to revitalize the soul of the one who was to be healed.'

As you enter your meditation, hold before you the image of the Great Healer. Focus not only on how he appears, but on the vibration which emanates from him and around him. Imagine what it would have been like to be in his physical presence, and know that he is with you now. *Lo, I am with you always....*

Meditation: THE CIRCULATING LIFE-FORCE

CLOSE YOUR eyes and your ears to all physical sight and sound, and see before you in imagery a path of white light. Move along this path, and you will notice it gently takes you up an incline, higher and higher, until you are above the earth—in the heavens—and you find yourself in a world of deep peace.

Before you is the round healing temple with the dome-shaped roof and white pillars supporting that canopy. You will find that the air you are breathing is rarefied and pure; and you are in an atmosphere of delicate colours.

You pass in between the two main pillars forming an entrance to go into this healing temple. There, in a golden radiance, is that pure white-robed figure of Jesus the Christ. Make your contact with him. Let us meditate on the figure before us.

You will feel the pulsation, the vibration of this powerful being. We feel and know that his life-force, his breath, is part of the lifestream which flows through the blood of the physical body. Now think of this pure life-force within the human circulation—circulating round your body. First of all in your own circulation, it commences in the heart and circulates all though you, your hands, your feet. Your whole body at this moment is exuding the healing power, and if you laid your hand on a patient the healing power would flow through that patient. This power you will carry with you whenever you attune yourself in the temple of healing to the one true source of healing power.

In the healing temple the Christ receives you now. Move up to him and kneel before him; his hands are placed upon you. Feel for yourself this blessing and dedication.

23. Developing Awareness of the Angels

WE WANT to help you to understand how you can be better channels for the Cosmic power, the Christ power, the angelic power. In healing, you do not work alone, whether you are a lone healer, a member of a group, or whether you are laying hands upon a sick person in a healing service. Never, never, never do you work alone. We want you to remember this.

You may see the angels of light with their wings around the patients. Do not think that this is a figment of your imagination, for we assure you that the angels' wings are very real. They are great rays of power and strength, and these wings can be enfolding and protecting. From them emanates the God-force. Angels work hand in hand with men and women, and you can develop your awareness and your fitness to be a clear and true channel of those angelic forces by communing with God each day, even if only for a short time. Just send your thanks to your Creator, and in the consciousness behind your active human brain dwell in the knowledge that the angels are with you, the heavenly hosts.

May every day of life find you opening the windows, not only of your house but of your soul—to let the sunlight flood you. You do not often see sunlight, you say; ah, there is invisible sunlight in the subtler atmosphere. So when you 'open' you will grow in wellbeing, in the power to love, in kindliness to life. As the power grows more potent, so you will become more assured as to this invisible force, its reality and effect.

When you can contact and receive these rays, you will gain

assistance from angel beings. We have previously spoken of angel beings specially concerned with building the form, with the perfecting of the physical body bodies of men and women. Hosts of such angels work in groups, under the direction of a great angel Lord. Although angels may appear to be impersonal, they are very strong in the particular quality or ray upon which they are serving, the ray which is a contribution to the whole Cosmos. By prayer and will, you create those colours in your aura that attract the angels.

'When you "open" you will grow in wellbeing, in the power to love, in kindliness to life. As the power grows more potent, so you will become more assured as to this invisible force, its reality and effect…. When you can contact and receive these rays, you will gain assistance from angel beings.'

Angels are beings of creation and of a love far more comprehensive that we can imagine. They respond to all the higher qualities of life. As you enter your meditation, imagine your guardian angel behind you, radiating towards you whatever quality you need at this time to enable you to raise your consciousness. You may see this radiation as a particular colour—for example, courage may show as gold, peace as blue, balance as green, love as rose, cleansing light as silver, comfort as pearl, wisdom as amethyst, and trust as violet.

Meditation: THROUGH THE HEALING WATER

OPEN YOUR inner vision, close your eyes to the physical and the material world in which you are confined, rise though the head chakra into a world limitless, a world of light, and you will find yourselves in a temple of living, pulsating light of limitless dimensions for it is a temple that fills the heavens.

There you will find yourself in the company of countless shining spirits who come to worship and to glorify their Creator. Tier upon tier, you will see the shining spirits. Into this great company all the sick and the poor and the sad can be brought by the ministering angels.

You are being brought by your ministering angel, at this very moment, into this glistening white temple in the heavens. In the centre of the great temple, in the arena, you will see a pool of blue liquid, the healing and cleansing pool, and you will see the gentle, humble, compassionate spirit of the Master Jesus and other healing masters who work with him.

You will see the angels of healing move down to touch the waters, disturbing the waters of the healing lifestream. Now the Master beckons you towards the steps that lead down into this pool of blue healing water; and your own particular healing angel will take you right through that healing water.

In the silence go through this real experience of being bathed in the healing pool of the Christ.... Use your imagination....

As you come up from the healing waters, you will be met by the figure of the Lord offering you the symbolic bread, the bread of life, and the golden wine which is the symbol of the spirit of Christ. Absorb the spiritual elements into your true self and the peace of God which passeth all understanding—of the earthly mind—will heal and bless you, and your feet will be on the road of Light.

24.
The Healer's Own Blessing

YOU ARE learning, every one of you, to become a bridge: a bridge between this world of darkness and the world of light. It is a great opportunity that has been shown to you, whether you are young or old in body. You have been presented with this opportunity to become a bridge between heaven and earth, and wherever you go, whomsoever you meet, remember that you are a bridge across which the angels travel, bringing the light and healing to the earth life. Is this not a comforting and a loving thought? Does it not make your life worthwhile, wherever you are, however humble you are? And we are going to say that the more humble and gentle and loving the man or woman, the purer is the channel.

You may not realize it, but every healer who comes to take part in the healing work, either in individual service or in a group, is being healed himself, or herself. You cannot make contact with this power without receiving your own blessing. You know, there is an ancient saying that every labourer is called into the temple to receive due payment for his or her work. At this very moment, you are called to the temple in spirit, to a very simple humble temple; and it is here that you receive your payment in a spiritual blessing and healing.

'Wherever you go, whomsoever you meet, remember that you are a bridge across which the angels travel, bringing the light and healing to the earth life.'

White Eagle has given us the image of the six-pointed Star as a symbol and focal point for the Christ rays. He also tells us that the Star, the Christ light, is within every heart. As you begin your meditation, focus on the centre of your chest, and imagine that perfect Star radiating there in all directions, to all life.

Meditation: RAYS OF HEALING FROM THE STAR

NOW, DEAR one, speaking of the Christ Light causes us to think of the perfect form of the Christ, for even as you have form, a physical body, so does every personality have a body, but the bodies vary in their etheric state. Some bodies are composed of very dense matter, dense ether; others are composed of a higher material substance, and so on.

We think of the Christ body as the perfect body, functioning perfectly and radiating the Light of heaven, which is the Light of the Christ Spirit operating through that body. This is the objective of all humanity.

We raise you in spirit to a higher plane, higher than the physical, to that beautiful land which is sometimes called the Summerland, because life is lived in Summer time and all is sunshine. The flowers are perfumed sweetly here and the birds are brightly feathered and sing with joy.

We are taken to this land, and we see it in our inner vision, in our imagination. We see the country all around, and on the apex of a hill we see the temple of healing. It is more than just white: it is all the colours of the rainbow, delicate colours. The main radiation is white and gold—yes, and silver—and then there are the blues and the mauves and the greens and the pinks, all intermingling, pulsating beautifully.

Let us approach first of all the steps leading up to this temple—broad white steps. Before we can approach the next flight of steps there is a pool or a bath of crystal water, and the angels wait for us, wait to receive us and guide us through this cleansing bath. The water does not wet us, only refreshes us and cleanses us from all earthly thoughts and emotions.

We approach the great door, the arch beautifully carved in stone. We go through the entrance and find ourselves in a vast building. We cannot estimate the dimensions of this vast temple of healing. Those who are weary in flesh are conducted to one or another of the alcoves all round this vast temple, where the couch is prepared for the body to lie upon it. All find rest and healing.

In the centre of the domed roof there is an immense Star. As a two-dimensional symbol it has six points, but in this higher dimension it has many more, even more than 144, and from each point there shines a ray of a different colour. The Star can be concentrated upon a bed, a couch, which lies immediately in the centre of this building. The patients are taken one by one and are led by the angels, the healing angels, to lie upon this couch. An order is given and there is an almost electric feeling. Then the Star turns and the light, the beam of light, pours upon the patient, particularly upon the head, at the brow centre, and then the heart and then the throat.

We are describing to you the true spiritual healing which everyone can have; both healer and patient can come under the power of that amazing Star and receive healing. For those who are sick and suffering, just tune yourselves, attune yourselves, to that perfect and glorious presence. The Christ presence is with you now. If you centre all your thoughts upon the Christ presence you may feel the touch. If you do not feel it upon your head or your shoulders or your hands, you will feel the warm golden Light of Christ pouring right through your body, animating, resuscitating all the atoms that are sick and weary.

Peace, the peace of God which is not of this world, fill your heart and heal your body, your soul and your mind. You can receive the full power of the Christ healing. God bless you.

25.
Pain will Pass

WE WOULD bring you into a closer awareness of the immortal truth that you only can live because you are a son or daughter of God. You are a seed of God sent forth from His–Her heart. Seek to remember your relationship to the divine love and wisdom which is your Creator. Not only is God the scientific law which governs, controls all life and keeps the stars in their course; God is also of humanity. We mean by this that God is like ourselves. He–She understands your heart and your need. Never think of God as a remote power watching the follies of humanity from afar. God is demonstrated to you through many world teachers, and most of all through Jesus, the Christ.

We know that each one of you has suffered. You have known grief and pain and anguish. You have suffered, and your suffering has been for you the pain of crucifixion. We know, also, because we have lived in a physical body, that it is a weak vehicle. We know that it gets tired and weary. We know how hard life can be for you. We feel your grief. We feel your pain. But, oh how we long to help you to realize that it is truly only transitory! It will pass.

Look up to the heavenly Father–Mother, and try to realize that the world of spirit is a very beautiful place, and moreover is all around you. We will give you a very slight illustration of this. Look at your springtime: the beauties of the spring flowers, the early leaves of trees, the green of the grass, the wonderful green of the shooting corn. Look at these beauties of nature (and those in whatever part of the world you live) and know that they are manifestations of the beauty of God's spirit. The brown earth does not produce these beauties alone, but has to be blessed and tended by the Creative Spirit; the brown earth, which is the symbol of the Great Mother and is the seedbed for all the gifts to human and animal life. But without the spirit of the heavenly Father, without divine energy and will, nothing could grow; nor could it grow without the command of God to the sunlight and the warmth, and to the wind currents, the air currents and the water currents, which causes the rain to come and bless the earth.

In just such a way, God will bring the flowers of joy out of pain. This message is to help you to find for yourself the peace and the beauty and the love of the Great Spirit. God is law, but God is also love. And this He–She demonstrated through the great initiate, Jesus, called the Christ. Christ is the light of the spiritual sun, not confined to any one individual: the light which is in the whole of humanity, waiting for each man and woman to open wide the gateway of their heart and their mind and receive into the heart, first of all, the conviction of God's love.

'Christ is the light of the spiritual sun, not confined to any one individual. It is the light which is in the whole of humanity....'

In the Buddhist tradition, the jewel in the heart of the lotus is symbolic of the ultimate place of stillness and self-awareness. To reach it means to transcend all suffering. To begin your meditation, focus on a still flame, whether literally or in your mind. Feel the sense of power contained there and at your command: the still point at your heart.

Meditation: THE JEWEL OF HEALING

CLOSE YOUR eyes, close your thoughts to all things earthly, and rise in vision and in spirit to the great white temple above, in the heights—though in spirit there is no distance and all time is eternal *now*. Concentrate and visualize the pathway, which is like a winding path right to the very apex of a mountain. The top of the mountain is ablaze with light. Visualize that winding path of light, which will take you right up beyond the clouds into that glorious sunlight: right up into the sun, the life-force, the creative power. There in that light you will see what will appear to you to be grand pillars supporting the invisible dome, and within that temple you will see a jewel; a most perfect crystal it will appear to you to be, and this jewel is sending forth all the rays of the cosmos. We will refer to it as the cosmic jewel of healing.

Supporting this jewel are the silent brethren, and through that crystal, which is like a magnifying glass would be to you, they look upon humanity with compassion. But they know, too, that humanity is on the upward path of spiritual evolution. We ask you now to enter this temple in the heights in stillness and silence.

Now we are in the temple. The dome is like a heavenly canopy—we are looking into heaven from the Star temple. All around us there are these Shining Ones, those who are working in spirit. Some of these are human beings, and some of them are angelic beings—human and angelic power combined. Create in your thoughts the purity and the simplicity and the grandeur and the beauty of this temple of healing. Absorb the peace and stillness.

Now, see with your inner vision the beloved Jesus. See him in his shining white garment with the radiation of sunshine and all the gentle colours of the spectrum pulsating in his aura. See his aura reaching out and penetrating the healing temple—be enveloped, yourself, in this pulsating spiritual life-force.

Be at peace and let your hearts beat in unison with the Divine Love that permeates every particle of the higher ether. 'I AM the truth and the Life.' His voice is heard giving you these words. *Behold I make all things new*—your minds, your bodies. 'I AM the Bread and the Wine of Life. Come, little one, take from me the heavenly bread and eat. Receive from me the heavenly wine. In the name of the Father–Mother and of the Son give yourselves to the Light.' The power of the Spirit of Christ will recreate you, and bring you to a realization of true healing. Every soul in this white temple receives the healing touch, and is blessed … blessed.

26. The Power of Healing Thought

IT DOES not matter who you are, sufficient that you are labouring to bring healing and light and peace to humanity. You are wielding a mighty power. If you sit in your home and pray earnestly for the help and upliftment of another soul, you are wielding a powerful influence. When you gather a group of people with combined thought on that one individual, you are multiplying that power ... and if you gather a continual chain of groups at work in the world, you are creating a mighty power which can overcome all enemies of good, and which can create a new earth.

There is need to know much concerning the power of thought. To pray is good. But to direct thought-power with precision and accuracy is quite different from prayer. In your work you first pray, you aspire to God, the Light of the World, and open your soul to the inflow of this Light and power. This is prayer. Then you use that which comes to you as the result of your prayer—you use the light, the power which fills your aura—and then as an individual or collective group you direct or focus this power of love. Your work in projecting this collective, harmonious thought is to assist individuals (nations or the world at large). You do not interfere with freewill, but you are assisting, even as sunshine from heaven helps flowers to blossom and send forth perfume.

Do you recognize the vital importance of each person realizing the purpose for which he or she was created, realizing his or her true son–daughtership with God, so that each person may be a healer of the nations? At this time in the world's history such healing is most vital. How can there be reconstruction of cities, reforming of nations, until this clear, crystal river of life, light and healing washes clean the world?

'If you sit in your home and pray earnestly for the help and upliftment of another soul, you are wielding a powerful influence.'

Think of the people you know, and the places in the world where there is need of healing. Do not think with anxiety or anguish, but try to think with compassion and dispassion. Dispassion does not mean you do not care—you care deeply—but it does mean that you allow the emotions to be calm. When the emotional body is at peace, the angels can draw close and use your thoughts of compassion in a powerful way for healing, a way which is almost beyond our understanding at the moment.

Meditation: THE LOVE WHICH HEALS

MAY YOUR soul be free from all earthly entanglements. Put forth the divine will from within your heart to free your mind from all earthly sorrows (disappointments, pain, anxieties) so that you may rise in consciousness to be with the Master in the temple of healing.

May you see with your inner eye what is prepared for you to see in the heaven world. The shining company, the angelic ones, are waiting to receive the souls of those who are asking to be healed. We see and we hope that you are able to see the bringing of the patients to the healing waters. At the appropriate time, the healing waters are touched by the power of the Lord. The patients are brought to the edge of the water and they pass though the healing pool with courage, with shining faces, and they are filled with healing of the Christ Spirit.

The beautiful landscape surrounding the healing temple is beyond earthly words to describe, but you will see for yourself the beauty of this spirit place. Bring those whom you wish to heal. Bring them in your thoughts, bring their souls to this healing pool and you may take them through it.

Love is the great healer, divine love. Love heals the bruised heart, the torn emotions, the heated brow. Love is the great healer and love personified is what you will see in the form of the Lord Christ. He comes into the heart of this healing ceremony. He comes in beauty, gentleness, stretching forth his hand to bless all people. 'I am the divine fire, the divine love which can never die and is never sick…. Come, dear one, and take the bread of life, for I give you sustenance, I give you new life.'

He holds the cup of wine…. 'The essence of my life is my spirit.' Drink. Feel the glorious fire flowing through you, cleansing and healing you from all confusion and pain. Be still and know that the Lord thy God is with thee.

27.
Breathing Practice: the Triangle of Light

THE PRACTICE of deep breathing is of great importance. In meditation groups we take great pains to help in the development of deep breathing. It should be practised daily. Never force deep breathing, however. Take it gently always. Remember to empty the lungs. Very few people properly empty their lungs. Correct breathing helps to steady the nerves and the emotional body, especially if the emotions are not under proper control. It will also help to clear congested parts such as the sinuses. If you are opening yourself to the Great White Spirit—that is, if your thoughts are expansive—you may imagine that you are out on the prairie and within the circle of the Great Spirits, the devas. As you think these things, you naturally want to fill yourself with light and air. Think along these lines, and you will find you will overcome shallow breathing.

Let us take the triangle, the symbol of the wisdom, love and power of God. Can you visualize this triangle of light? Can you think of it as established in your heart? Most people think only with the mind or brain. But you can learn to think with your heart. Try this, transferring your thought to the heart. Quietly conceive this triangle of wisdom, love and power as established there. You should feel aspiration instantly. You may think dispassionately, but you cannot think coldly from the heart. We suggest that you will receive great help from making a daily practice of thinking in your heart of the triangle of light. Become aware, and know that you have placed it there.

We were speaking about the intake of light, the breathing in of sunlight, or the Christ light which revivifies and strengthens. Our next step is to breathe this light into the heart. The symbol of the triangle will make a magnetic point of attraction. Sit, then, with spine erect, yourself the apex of the triangle. Instantly you become aware of the Sun and of the Christ spirit permeating this Sun. You will feel the in-pouring of light through the triangle and in time it will be burning in your heart—'a flaming heart', we have heard it called.

It takes sometimes many incarnations to get the heart really aflame with the divine love. Human love is a passionate love and prejudiced; divine love is a threefold love, for divine love gives birth to wisdom, and love and wisdom give birth to power. You cannot love divinely without being wise, and you cannot love wisely without becoming a centre of power. This means a spirit that is tender, wise in every worldly, mental and spiritual detail, and a body, soul and spirit poised, radiantly healthy, knowing only the light.

Those suffering from various little ills can put into practice these exercises. Bring in, into the apex of this triangle, the glowing vibrant light, the life-force. If you can hold it steadily and unflinchingly and get it circulating throughout your being, you will be healed.

Beloved children of earth, according to your belief and your faith be it unto you. Breathe in the breath, the holy breath. God the Father knows your heart. The joy and love you feel in this communion is only an infinitesimal part of that great joy and love which you will know in time. Let this encourage you to keep on keeping on in spite of difficulties. Do not battle with difficulties; just let them fall behind you.

To those of you who are weary with the journey, we would say, Look up! Try to live above the turmoil and the distress of the earthly emotions. Look up into the world which is all light, your true home. God knows your need and in due time every need will be supplied according to God's love.

'It takes sometimes many incarnations to get the heart really aflame with the divine love. Human love is a passionate love and prejudiced; divine love is a threefold love, for divine love gives birth to wisdom, and love and wisdom give birth to power.'

In order to get the inner feeling of the triangle of light, first feel how you are sitting. You are making a shape similar to a pyramid, particularly if you sit cross-legged, with the crown of your head at the apex. As you do this you feel foursquare on your chair or on the earth—centred, upright and perfectly poised to receive the light. No matter what your body looks like, or how it feels, you can get the inner feeling of being balanced, so that all the energies set in motion by your breathing practice can flow easily within and through you.

Meditation:
THE PERFECT BREATH

May you be raised into the heavenly places. May you know the Presence, the almighty Presence with you. Lack of ease, dis-ease, is the result of something being out of place in your position, the position you have taken in life. If you open yourselves to the sacred and secret harmonies, you will be healed, adjusted.

Take this picture in your mind's eye: the blue healing lake in the midst of the temple gardens with the shining angels receiving each patient, taking them through the blue healing stream. Breathe in the holy breath, the perfect breath of life, breath it in. Breathe out the blessing of love. Practise this rhythm of holy breathing, breathing in the life of the Creator. Let it flow through your whole being, harmonizing, adjusting, purifying, ennobling your whole life.

Sit erect. Think of the triangle. Let it be a living thing in your heart. Be still. With every inhalation the light enters, with every exhalation you bless and you love. You live, you breathe, you have your being in this divine life-force. No harm can ever come near you, for you are encircled, the divine light enfolds you. Think of this every morning, be conscious of it as much as you can during your day's work; and each day will bless you and enrich those you love and serve.

When you go to sleep at night, let your last thought

be of praise and thankfulness to God. Think of the world of light and of crossing the river to the other side, to the world of light. Direct yourself by the divine will that is within you. Let it be your director in your sleep and in your waking. Do not look about you on the earth plane for inharmony and for those who hurt you or who are rough and unkind. Look above them. Keep your thoughts always fixed upon the good, the true and the beautiful God-life. Breathe in the breath of God. Breathe out the blessing of love and healing upon the earth. You, the child of God, you are whole, you are *holy, holy, holy*; and as you think so you become.

God has created you, man or woman, in His–Her own image: that is, with the same qualities of spirit and form. *Be ye perfect as your father in heaven is perfect.* Say this to yourselves every morning: 'I am perfect as my Father created me perfect. I am divine Love. I am divine peace'.

28. One Universal Life

JESUS REPEATED what so many other great world teachers have said: 'Do unto others what you would like to have them do unto you.' This is the law. And he said, *Thou shalt love the Lord thy God.* Love this infinite power, love and wisdom. Love God with all your heart and your soul, and your neighbour as yourself—which means that you live every day and every minute of your life conscious that you are living in God, in the heavenly state of love. All creatures are of God and belong to this one grand universal life from which no atom, no tiny heart can be separated. You are all one in this divine Spirit.

We would have you understand that you cannot isolate yourselves from the rest of humanity. In a practical sense you will prove this to be true, if you give thought to your dependence upon countless other human beings for your daily needs.

We want to convey the idea, the truth, that you are at this very moment completely linked with all created beings; you are one in the vast ocean of spirit. This is a basic truth which all humanity will in time come to understand. We want you to feel, in your own soul, this eternal truth.

Every one of you will in time receive that flash of consciousness in which you will know for certain that you are one in the whole, that you are part of the whole, that you are part of God; and that in God are all men, women and creatures. You are part of that infinite and eternal life from which all form at the physical level has proceeded. This is true, and it is a grand thought that however humble you feel you are, you are one in the Infinite Spirit; and that in that vast ocean of life you live and have your being. All creatures and all beings, irrespective of religion or race, are one in God.

'You are at this very moment completely linked with all created beings; you are one in the vast ocean of spirit.... Every one of you will in time receive that flash of consciousness in which you will know for certain that you are one in the whole, that you are part of the whole, that you are part of God....'

As a prelude to meditation, you may like to contemplate nature. Perhaps you can actually wander outside, or even simply observe a houseplant, or a tree from your window. As you do so, breathe consciously and imagine that you are breathing with that natural form; that you are both breathing in God, breathing out the light of love.

Meditation: FOLLOWING THE FLIGHT OF THE DOVE

LOOK UP to the eternal light and love, and let it flow through you and recreate and transform your soul and your body. Breathe in the life of God as it manifests in nature: in the trees, the earth, the sky. Feel your oneness with this life.

Now there appears in the white ether above you a white bird, a pure white dove, which is the symbol of the Holy Spirit. Let us follow it in its flight.

We leave the earth … and we find that we are entering the Great White Temple, not built by people, but built by the angels in heavenly spheres. You will hear the music of the spheres and see the countless souls, all in pure white raiment following the flight of the white dove into this heavenly temple.

Feel the hush and the enveloping power and the wondrous love and peace, the at-one-ment that each soul feels with the others—at-one-ment because of the love of the Son that envelops you all. They chant in a spiritual language: 'The Father and I are one, and the great Mother of human kind is one with me. I am in the light. I give light. And I bless and raise all people up into the light.'

Oh, the wonderful love that fills your being as you move forward towards the Lord Christ, who is waiting for you! He knows every individual, and you are enfolded in his radiance, his aura … perfect, perfect, perfect in your life, in your soul body. In your soul body you know him. You are filled, filled with this life-force, this white magic, this white fire. You are alight—you are healed. The peace of the Christ spirit is upon you.

29.
The Tree of Life

THE TEMPLES and structures of old were built upon the formation of the trees. Trunk and branch taught the builders the secrets of pillar and vault and groin. The harmonies of the universe find expression in the trees, as in your own body; and in the architecture of the temples of old you can find expressed in miniature the Grand Temple of the Universe.

You contain within yourself the Tree of the Knowledge. The spine can be likened to the trunk; and the two aspects of life, positive and negative, rise up from the roots of the spine, blossom forth from the head and bring forth fruit. One can see in the circulatory system of the body, its stem, its branches, its intricate network, a veritable Tree of Life. We see the possibilities for you all—of your growth and regeneration. Ultimately we see the human tree, most beautiful of all, beneath whose wide branches of compassion and understanding humanity can shelter, and whose fruits of love and wisdom humanity can find.

You can look with the outer eye at a wood, and trees, and say, 'How beautiful!'. On the other hand, you may be overcome by the glory of the wood's inner life. It is all there, but usually your inner eyes are tight shut; but you may catch a flash, or as you will say 'imagine'. You may not yet able to make conscious contact with all these Invisibles, but you are being prepared. Slowly your souls are unfolding the truth which is within you. You are as a tree in the heavenly garden. Through your root the sap, the white light, rises into the tree, and the tree sends forth branches into which the sap and life-force flows. Stand in worship at the foot of our brothers the trees; raise your hearts to the heavens, and hear the sounds, the music, the harmonies of the universe, wafting through the branches.

In imitation of the great Lord Buddha, let us assemble under the canopy of heaven, shaded by the branches of the universal Tree of Life—God—and absorb His–Her blessing of peace. We *are* those trees....

'Slowly your souls are unfolding the truth which is within you. You are as a tree in the heavenly garden.'

The meditation that follows is very much about the healing to be found in nature, and the importance of our contact with that natural life. To become one with that inner life of nature we need to feel the great love of the master soul, like the Buddha, or Jesus. To begin your meditation, feel your spine is like a strong treetrunk, with the light rising up and flooding your heart with love for all life.

Meditation: AT ONE WITH ALL LIFE

LET US strive, then, with God's love in our hearts, never to hurt our beloved companions, human, animal, insect or bird…. May we enter into the spirit of brotherhood with all flowers and trees; feeling with them, becoming part of them … one grand brother–sisterhood of light.

Beloved, rise now in spirit … and we enter a natural sanctuary of healing in the world of spirit. In the centre behold the presence…. Jesus … with the birds all gathered around him, at his feet, resting on his head and shoulder and hands. Behold, he stands in your midst, and the lion and the lamb, the eagle and the robin and the dove are all around … and the lily, pure white … and the rose…. He stands upon meadowland that is carpeted with the simple flowers of the wild places. Behold the running water, trickling down the mountainside, and then rushing forward, a river, towards the sea….

Now the stars shine through the blue canopy, and the sun and the moon together blend their light. May the brotherhood of all life sing in your soul. As now you rise to the mountaintop to gaze upon the golden sun as it sinks over the horizon, you know eternal peace and at-one-ment. You know that your feet are set upon a path that will lead unfailingly to the eternal happiness you seek.

You descend once more to the temple garden and

listen to the singing of birds, the language of our animal brethren; to the music of the flowers that comes to your senses in perfume and colour. The waving grasses invite you to rest…. Rest….

This is the life of the spirit. God has provided these things for our happiness. Strive to live in spirit, when you can, and bring through into the physical life the inspiration of the true life that is yours.

30.
Evolution

THERE ARE many groups in the world today, both great and small, which are at work under the direct control, power or guidance of the Master's mind, through his disciples both incarnate and discarnate. The masters are ever seeking channels through which to pour their light, their wisdom to humanity.

A master looks out upon the world and sees it dark, but in the darkness shine certain stars—those who are ready to be used in service. So as soon as your light shines clearly enough to be observed by the Master or his disciples, so surely then you are drawn into his service.

When a master desires to manipulate physical matter, which is what you are trying to do when you heal, the master is always silent—and holds, in his or her thought, God. A master flows into God. He or she enters into the heart of God. The power is then in his or her God-thought to manipulate the very cells, physical cells or even the material cells, the cells in matter.

We would remind you, once again, of the power of thought, the thought of God, the thought of the higher mind, the concentration on thoughts of love and healing, which have a powerful effect upon the cells of the physical body, upon every activity of life in the physical body.

'A master flows into God. He or she enters into the heart of God. And the power is then in his or her God-thought to manipulate the very cells, physical cells or even the material cells, the cells in matter.'

Contemplate what tenderness means to you. You may choose, for example, to visualize a small baby, or a young animal, or someone you love. Let that sense of loving, which involves being quite vulnerable, arise within you and rest in the feeling. As you do this your heart chakra opens—this is the balance point of all the chakras; the place where love enters and brings harmony to every part of your body.

Meditation: THE FRAGRANCE OF THE ROSE

NOW, LET us forget the earth. You are going to a real place. You are going into the healing temple, which is built of pure white substance, pure light. It is scintillating with colour. Try and imagine it and see all round you in a wide circle the spirit healers. Over the altar is a symbol, the cross within the circle of light or love, one of the most ancient symbols of protection.

From the centre of that cross we first see a beautiful rose—a live, beautiful rose—the perfume is sweet, fragrant, heavenly. You feel the rose, the fragrance of the rose, going right into your heart. From this centre—from the rose—there gradually comes forth a tiny form, like a baby, the Christ-child. It grows into a perfect human form created by the Father–Mother God. It is the Light, the Christ love, the great being who understands you; who comes so close to you, right into your heart, so that you too can feel love and compassion for suffering, and for ignorance, and for those who hurt you.

This is the love that can save every soul, which can raise even atoms of the earth itself. And now we can hear the very stones singing, singing the notes in the universe, singing the beautiful music of all nature. The stones, and the very earth itself, are singing in praise.

You are blessed.

31.
Divine
Harmonies

BELOVED brethren, we bring to you peace, the peace of heaven; we bring the peace of God to your heart. We would like to explain to you that in the higher spheres of life (or shall we say, just beyond the dark veil of materialism) we listen to the voices of our earthly brethren and hearing them brings to us great joy and happiness. We listen to the music of our brethren on earth—the musical instruments and above all the music of the heart—which we hear but you may not. But when you learn to withdraw from the noise and bustle of the world and enter into your own inner sanctuary, you will develop that sensitive hearing which will enable you to hear the music of nature, the music of the tiniest bird, the music that is in the air.

Just think of it, the music in the rippling water, in the gentle breeze, in the shaking of the leaves of the trees! When we were living in a physical body, we lived with a company of our people who were taught from childhood to listen to the voice of the Great White Spirit, to listen to the voice of the angels in the trees, in the rustle of the leaves and in the breezes. We were taught to listen quietly and intensely to catch the music of life, the music that was so healing, so harmonious.

In the silence, you listen and hear the music of heavenly spheres, the music of nature, of the wind in the trees, the song of the birds, the gentle murmur of the voices of the ferns and flowers, and even the murmur of the blades of grass. You must learn to be still, and to listen to God's voice, which is showing that all are one in the spirit—*all one.*

If you can think of God not as complete and separate, but as a vast company which is also a oneness, or a vast life which also is an intelligent and controlling principle of life, if you can break through that feeling or that sense of the individuality, into the infinite power and light that flows through to you, then you will do your finest work. Not only will you be able to help individuals, you will be able to help the whole world, all life; because you will be allowing God to flow through you.

'When you learn to withdraw from the noise and bustle of the world to enter into your own inner sanctuary, you will develop that sensitive hearing…. You must learn to be still, and to listen to God's voice, which is showing that all are one in the spirit—*all one*.'

As you sit to meditate, imagine you are drawing yourself inward—drawing all the threads of your thinking and life towards the centre. Focus on the centre of your being, imagining your spine like 'a rod of light'. Once you have found that still centre of your self away from the everyday mind, then you can imagine flowing out beyond the confines of the self, without losing the self. You can imagine being one with all life, yet still individual and unique.

Meditation: THE SPIRIT WORLDS

WE WOULD raise your conscious mind, your soul, far above the earth. We draw you up to your true home, to a spirit world of light and beauty; of flower-filled gardens and vast parklands with beautiful lakes, upon which there float lily blooms. We take you to the gentle flowing rivers with the clear water, through which you can look and see the many-coloured stones and the water life. We show you soft green banks covered with small flowers. We take you through gardens ablaze with the various coloured blooms.

We show you children playing with large, transparent balls like bubbles. We see the children swinging in the trees, which are spring trees filled with blossom; for the children are in the springtime of life.

We take you to the temples of healing, where souls are being gently restored to vigour and confidence in God's life and God's power to sustain that life; and to bear all the problems and responsibilities of the children of God. Now we want to take you to the temple of the Sun. Imagine that we are raised in spirit and stand in a Grecian temple of the past, but built of the finest spiritual substance and pulsating with light and spiritual power.

You may see columns that rise up right out of sight, supporting (it would seem) a heavenly canopy. There in our midst is the pedestal upon which the great Master stands. He is radiating heavenly love. His love is pouring upon you, upon all of us … and we feel that we are wrapped around by his sunlit aura.

We feel comforted, healed. We are in the centre of simple wisdom. Wisdom is ever simple, and it is always found where there is love—love which gives, which serves; love which has no thought except for God and God's children.

32.
The Gift of Light

LIGHT is a generally accepted gift, indeed the great gift of life. For where there is no light, there is no life. Light *is* life. What a great gift then is light! Light penetrates the darkest places. Sunlight searches out the dark places, and reveals beauty, restores health. Look through a magnifier at a butterfly's wing, or some tiny flower in the hedge, and what do you see?—the most exquisite colour, delicacy, and beauty. Without the rays of light, such beauty would not exist for you.

You desire a means of destroying disease? Then open your windows to the air, to the sunlight, and go out into the sunlit air yourself. Sunlight is the great purifier; many instances could be given of the cleansing properties of light. Medical men and women are now using healing methods new to the modern world, but well-known to the ancients.

Let us then try to understand how great a gift is light. Sunlight, the white light, can be subdivided into the seven colours of the spectrum. The seven colours are permeating every form of life on earth, and each has its vibration; even the herbs used for healing, according to the influence of the planet which causes their growth, reflect certain vibrations of colour. It is the vibration from these herbs, when introduced into the physical body, which cause the readjustment from inharmony to harmony. Disease is lack of ease, lack of harmony.

Behind and interpenetrating the physical sun is the spiritual Sun. It is also the Son, the Christ, or Child of the Father–Mother God.

Thus we can see how effective the Christ light or the thought of the Christ spirit can be in the healing of a person's sick body. By attuning ourselves to the all-pervading Cosmic Christ, we open up the channel to receive these healing rays.

'You desire a means of destroying disease? Then open your windows to the air, to the sunlight, and go out into the sunlit air yourself.'

To begin your meditation, imagine that you are sitting in the sunlight. Feel the warmth of the sun pouring down upon you and through you, melting all tension and depression. Have the thought in your mind that this sunlight is the Light of God, and it has the power to transform all darkness, whether physical, mental or emotional, into more love and light.

Meditation: VISUALIZING THE COLOUR RAYS

TO STRENGTHEN your ability to visualize or imagine the colours used in healing, it is quite a good idea to create in your mind a picture to which you can turn for inspiration.

For instance, in your imagination go to the shore of a lake, just at sunrise. Feel the hush, the waiting hush of all nature as the light begins to shine from the horizon. Feel this rising sun deep within your own being; feel its rays shining on the water.

The sun is filling the sky and the water with glorious colour, and right in the heart of that blazing light can be glimpsed a human form, the shining form of the Great Healer.

From the heart of the sun, under the direction of the Healer, and along the straight beams of light, emerge the angels of healing. These are the angels of the soul qualities, qualities which we shall all eventually build into our solar bodies.

See the light and colour of each angel reflected in the mirror-like surface of the water, until the whole lake consists of pools of different coloured light, each under the care—under the radiance—of its own angel.

As you watch these heavenly sun-colours reflected in the mirror of the lake, choose one. Feel yourself drawn to one of the colour pools. Remember the colours are all pure and sunlit, nothing dark, nothing murky—just radiant light!

33. The Miracle of Healing

THE GENTLENESS of the spirit is the power you all have within you to perform miracles. What is a miracle? A miracle is a manifestation that cannot be understood by physical law. It is outside physical law. But it is the operation of a spiritual law. There is no explanation for a miracle at the ordinary level of thought, of intellect, for it is beyond the intellect to comprehend. Also, a miracle does not necessarily take place in a flash. It sometimes takes a little time for the God-power to work.

There are different forms of healing. You can heal by touch, but only when you have made the contact from your heart chakra, which is like a flower branching from the spinal cord. When you make that contact, and breathe in the life and the light of your Creator, you are filled, filled with miraculous healing power. Or when you sit in a group or alone, you immediately pray to that same infinite divine love, and are filled with love, compassion, sympathy. Pray for understanding of the disturbance in your patients that works through the nervous system and manifests as illness. The spinal cord is the stalk, shall we call it, of the thousand-petalled lotus at the crown of the head. As you love and pray, that thousand-petalled lotus opens like a flower to the sunlight, and the sunlight is the creative power of God.

Healing does not only take place through the healing touch of the hand. The basis of all healing is love. The Lord Jesus, the Christ, said: *Love one another*. That is all. This love in your heart—compassion, pity if you like—but still *love*: this word 'love' is the one that attracts the magic power, the power of the Lord Christ—or if you prefer, the Christ Light. In the Christ Light you will find all the colour rays that are needed in your healing work. Be conversant with the supreme light and you will have no weariness of mind and body. You will be very vibrant because life more abundant will continually flow into you. It may sound simple, but it is not easy. But it has been said, 'To thine own self be true'; if you are true to yourself, to your higher self, you are making contact with the Christ spirit.

When you are in doubt, confusion, seek your own inner sanctuary, the sanctuary of your heart. Visualize your surroundings in the spirit sphere of life, in a small white and gold chapel. Stand quite alone, and wait. Then go upon your knees and listen to the music of the spheres, to the voice of Christ. He will not mislead you. Train yourself in this, this entering your own white chapel, until it becomes even more real to you than any physical form that you are accustomed to. Go into the heavenly silence; wait for the heavenly music; listen for His comforting, wise guidance.

'The spinal cord is the stalk, shall we call it, of the thousand-petalled lotus at the crown of the head. And as you love and pray, that thousand-petalled lotus opens like a flower to the sunlight, and the sunlight is the creative power of God.'

As you begin your meditation, feel the uprightness of your etheric spine, with all the chakras as White Eagle has described them, flowers upon the stalk, and the crown open to the sunlight of God. Imagine being in the presence of the Great Healer right now, in your room. Feel his aura around you, and the indescribable essence of his love, beyond all emotion, which flows through you. He gathers you into his presence. He lifts you up; he brings you into his peace.

Meditation: THE GREAT HEALER

BELOVED, look up! Look up in spirit. We ask you to leave aside the material world and the perplexities and anxieties of your incarnation. Remember that you come from a home of peace and light and beauty. You are attached to that home.

Put aside all misunderstanding and confusion and go straight to the heart of truth, to the heart of God your Father–Mother. As you surrender your will to God, and have faith and confidence in the love of God, so that love will work out in your lives.

At this moment, rise with your vision on the hilltops, on the higher life, and go straight towards it. We know how hard it is for you when your bodies are tired and out of tune, but there is the will within you to bring your body into tune with the harmony of God.

We are going to ask you to follow us into the heights. We are going to take you to a place where there is a ring of high places on the etheric level. In the world below there is much conflict, sorrow, sickness and fear. But at this level, in the mountaintops, we see only the form of Jesus clothed in shining white apparel. The expression on his face is all love—all love.

Now he begins to rise and we rise with him, leaving the earth level behind us as we rise into a higher state of life. You are with him at a higher level of life. In the silence and the stillness you are with God….

In the temple of prayer and communion the Master comes to you; and in your own temple, your own private chapel, where you kneel before the altar. You kneel in his presence, and he, being all love, understands your need. He offers to you the wine. He offers the cup. Take, in your spirit; sip the wine—his spirit, his life. Sip it; absorb it. It is his life, his power, his beauty, his gentleness and love. 'My life which is given for you.' He means that he lives in you and for you, and this is the source of your strength. Whatever ordeal lies before you, remember the Christ presence, for it will never leave you. It brings peace and courage. *Lo! I am with you always.*

34.
Communion with the Christ Spirit— the Sun

WE HAVE before us as an example one who is known as Christ, a physical embodiment of a great and gracious spirit ... and we see a manifestation of this beautiful spirit in lesser forms in men and women. Therefore, as we contact him it gives us hope, it raises us to a higher level of consciousness, for we feel through our communion with this Christ spirit a strength and inward conviction that what he has accomplished all the sons and daughters of God may yet accomplish. When it becomes alive through contact with this supreme light of life, the soul is filled with fire and courage, the body is drawn erect and the head reaches heavenward, and the feet which tread the earthly path become strong in their purpose.

This, we know, is the way of truth. This, we know, is the secret of a healthy life. Healthy means holy, and holy means healthy. We would set our hearts upon the supreme goal, Christ, and would open our hearts to receive and to give forth the harmonies of heaven.

Do not think, beloved friends, that all this is impractical. Put yourselves into harmony, into tune with spiritual law, and every need of body, soul and spirit will be supplied. And what is this law? Divine love...! Keep your heart full of divine and gentle love ... and then difficulties fall away, sorrow recedes into the background, and you cannot help but know the gentle presence of your Master.

However hard the task, however bitter your heart may feel, and even if you feel mortally hurt by the apparent injustice in your life, try to put aside your hurt and surrender to the all-wise and all-loving God. Try to imagine that the Lord Christ is with you as you picture him—gentle and kind and loving. You will feel his love penetrating your heart, irradiating your soul, and you will feel at peace. The nervous system will lose its strain; the bloodstream will be purified; you will be giving yourself a healing treatment. Of your own volition you call upon and make contact with the higher self and the life-force. Thus the light of the Christ, the Sun, will flow into you and you will feel it as a warm glow, irradiating your whole system. Do this in the morning, at noon, and again at night before you sleep. Try it, and you will learn the secret of the universe, for this is true communion with Christ.

The peace which is beyond the understanding of the world enters, and the Christ it is who says: *My peace I leave with you... my peace I give unto you.*

'Keep your heart full of divine and gentle love … and then difficulties fall away, sorrow recedes into the background….'

It is often hard to become still at the beginning of a meditation. The important thing is not to be disheartened or guilty when the mind seems restless, but rather to keep drawing your attention back to the stillness of the body and the rhythm of the breath. The image of a still lake is perfect for focusing the thoughts. If you can, imagine the depth and pure colour of the water. The surface gradually becoming unruffled, and as reflective as glass. Think of that mystical time just as the sun rises on a still summer morn with the water suffused with gold and rose light. A scene like this can bring such a sense of harmony that one becomes still without realizing it….

Meditation: REST IN STILLNESS

BE STILL, and know God…. If your soul can rest in stillness like a deep, clear pool of water, it may reflect the picture of heaven, the picture of Christ. Let us feel, let us know his joy.

When you pass onward into the world of light, you will be wholly conscious of God's love, beauty, power and creation. You will use your mind-power then to hold in place forms of indescribable beauty—a condition of life and a power which is being born within you now.

So let peace dwell in your souls, and may your souls acquire the stillness of a perfect lake. Nothing matters in life except this. You will lose nothing, nor will any opportunity be neglected for you to make progress, and more than this you will give abundantly to others. So let the peace dwell in your heart and the light of heaven shine in you, as the light shines on the still water.

And now there stands before you a majestic figure—so tall and noble, so shining with pure white light. The face shines with love and the eyes look into your heart with tender compassion. This is truth. He is all truth. He loves you, because he sees in you that shining light, that jewel, which is part of himself.

His hands are raised to bless you … and the rays of light fall from his hands, from the tips of his fingers…. They pierce and strengthen your heart, for he gives you courage, and joy, and peace.

35. The Brother–Sisterhood of All Life

THERE ARE many groups working for brotherhood. Once they thought just of the brotherhood and sisterhood of human beings, but groups now rightly teach the brotherhood of animals, of nature, of the trees and the flowers, and the clouds and the wind, of all creation.

As we gaze over the earth, we see groups striving everywhere to encourage the love of nature. Consciously or unconsciously, the young people are learning, are communing with their brothers the trees, with brother sunlight, and with their sisters the flowers, and the birds.

The brother–sisterhood of man and woman and the animal kingdom! If you love the creatures given life by God, it is impossible to be cruel, to slay wantonly, indeed to shed their blood, unless in cases of sheer necessity. Then they are serving you in the only way they can serve, by giving up life itself. But with so many healthful and pure foods as an alternative, is it necessary to eat your brother animal, your sister bird?

It all comes to this: your consciousness is gradually being raised to a plane of universal brother–sisterhood, the plane whereon all people will know that they cannot say a word of unkindness against those they walk with without hurting themselves. Humanity will realize that all creation is one vast community of spirit, one atom inseparable from another. In this great family all are held in the love and the power of the divine spirit, our Father–Mother God.

The Great White Light of God, shining behind and through all, is the only reality. All else is illusion. Serve others by calling forth the tiny light implanted within each breast; do what you can to relieve the sufferings of the oppressed everywhere; work for the obliteration of cruelty to all animals. Live yourself a pure and simple and humble life, judging no-one, but loving all.

Let us do our very best to refrain from hurting any living creature. This is love. If there is something that has to be said, which said in one way would be hurtful, try to choose the other, the loving way. Say it gently; give a great deal of thought to it, and put it in the kindest and most loving way. A slash with a sword can be painful!

The inner urge to love will naturally bring a shrinking from hurting any form of life.

'The inner urge to love will naturally bring a shrinking from hurting any form of life.'

As you begin your meditation, take your thoughts to a time in the past when you have walked among tall trees, or imagine how it would be to do so. Recreate in your thoughts a feeling of uprightness, of drawing yourself erect, so that your spine feels straight; your feet and lower chakras are well-grounded and your higher chakras and the crown chakra are open to the light. The heart is then released....

Meditation: THE TEMPLE AMONG THE PINES

RELAX all tenseness, be at peace and commune with God within your heart, for God dwells in all things, and is expressed in beauty throughout the universe: in nature, and by the brotherhood of people and angels, in our brethren the animals, and in all the worlds of nature.

Enter with us into the spheres of true love. Seek the stillness in the tranquillity of nature ... in a natural temple among the tall pines; stand in the presence of the great powers of the spiritual realms, and absorb the love that is pouring upon you....

It is the love—infinite, universal, and abundant—from which you came, and that which you are. The whole purpose of life is that you shall realize this beauty and this love, and by continuing to express it, grow, grow, *grow* in the perfection of the God-life that dwells within you and from which you were born.

Call upon the angels of love, our brethren of the angelic spheres, to minister to your waiting heart. In the peace and stillness within your soul, worship the giver of life, be thankful for the glory of the earth, for open skies, sunlight and gentle rain; for the recurring seasons of the year, for the affection and companionship of the animal world, for the fragrance and beauty of the flowers and, above all, for the consciousness of Christ.

May this consciousness grow stronger; the Christ, both without and within your soul.

May the peace of the eternal love be with you.

36.
When Facing a Challenge

IF YOU FEEL a little weary sometimes, try to remember that the power of love from the Great Spirit is infinite. It will come to you without fail as you humbly enter into the temple of the heart, which is within your own inner self and is there for everyone—though not everyone knows it. As you become simple as a child, trusting as a child, you are filled with the power which heals.

What we are trying to explain is that deep within your heart is the silence. This is where you make the link with the infinite and eternal creative force. It is like a jewel. It radiates through your aura, it projects through your hands and through every centre of your body. When you enter a room you carry your healing, or God's healing, with you. Try not to separate yourself at any time from this power. Let it be a living force in you.

Whatever your calling, whatever your vocation, whether it is a simple one, or a more public vocation, whenever you yourself feel strained, or perhaps a little nervous of the work you have to do; if you have to lecture, if you have to perform music, if you have to use your voice or if you have to use your brain or hands in any capacity, always carry with you an awareness of this jewel in your heart, because it is a magnet. It is not only a magnet for the spiritual forces to draw close to you, it is also a magnet in the world.

It does not matter where you go, or what is your vocation, if you will just think of this shining jewel within your heart, it immediately draws to you creative power. Then the angels who are working with you on the particular ray upon which you are called to work draw close to you. But we would like you to realize also that God and his angels never force their way into the privacy of another soul. The soul has to open his or her heart in love, and then the angels come to you and you are filled with the power of the spirit.

'Deep within your heart is the silence. This is where you make the link with the infinite and eternal creative force.'

It is not always easy to become aware of the silence within. The mind clamours with all sorts of thoughts as soon as you close your eyes! White Eagle tells us that one way to clear your thought-atmosphere is to chant the *Aum* a few times before you begin your meditation. Make sure you will not be disturbed, and focus solely on the sound, remembering as you do so that it is the Word of God—a holy sound. When you finish, the ensuing change from sound to silence will increase the awareness of that silence, and so you can begin to be aware of a deeper absence of sound which is complete stillness.

Meditation:
HEALING FROM THE DIVINE FIRE

LET US enter the temple of healing, with its great pillars and perfectly-shaped domed roof. We raise your consciousness and take you higher. We want you to realize that as you approach the altar you are being filled, filled with the eternal fire. It is the fire, the fire on the altar that we direct your attention to and the Star above it is your focal point. As you gaze at that Star you realize its implications, uniting you, the microcosm, with the macrocosm … cosmic consciousness—you are in IT. You gaze into that Star and you will see the base, upon which is erected the triangle—the perfect pyramid. This is the symbol of the cosmos, the divine fire, the symbol of all healing work.

Concentrate upon the divine fire, symbolized in that Star; feel the enfolding canopy of the heavens. Feel the power drawing you to the table of communion, the altar. You receive more than the bread and the wine, you receive the divine fire, so that instead of being weary and feeling sick and ill, you feel the fire is your life, the life-force of all created beings—the force which works in nature, which animates and gives life to all creatures.

When you look up at the sky and you look at the countless stars, remember that Star which is your destiny. Every effort you make to immerse yourself in spiritual service, spiritual thought, spiritual ideal, is a step forward on your path.

Once again, concentrate upon that blazing golden altar with the divine fire burning upon it, and the power and light pouring down upon that fire from the Star, the symbol of eternity and eternal life. If you think on these things, you will find that the power for your healing will pour into you. You are a channel. Hold fast to that thought and you will lose all weariness, all fear. You will surrender, resign yourself to that infinite and eternal power of your Creator. That is the true healer who can feel like this. Don't let this part (pointing to the brain) interfere with you, just open your heart to that love, because the Star is your focal point and symbol of divine fire, divine love.

37.
The Most Effective Action

WE OFTEN hear the question: 'How can I help my friend in hospital other than by thought and meditation?' But we would tell you that the power of thought is *more* effective than the power of speech or the written word.

You can help your friend by continual, habitual, constructive thought, by sending out optimistic, good, constructive thought. Take your friend in thought to the great Mother and to the Christ. Persist in this. The healing rays sent by thought, we assure you, are as effective as any physical ministration, and more effective in many cases.

Also, if what you call the worst happens (for you, we think, the worst is for a soul to pass out of the physical body) try always to remember that the soul, far from dying or having need for your grief, sorrow and pity, is being released into a world of infinite beauty, love and joy. It does not die. As the great American poet wrote, death is 'the angel sent To draw the unwilling bolts and set us free'.* When the time comes for the body to be laid aside, the spirit is still near you. Where there is love there is no separation. The spirit of the one left behind merges with the released spirit. The law of harmony prevails, the law of reunion and mergence. The two come together as one.

Yes, earth life is a hard school, but you will not find it so hard if you draw aside the curtain and live conscious of the limitless spiritual life.

*James Russell Lowell

'The healing rays sent by thought, we assure you, are as effective as any physical ministration, and more effective in many cases.'

Entering meditation need not be unusual—it can be likened to kicking your shoes off at the end of a busy day and feeling that no-one now expects anything of you, that you can do what you wish. As you enter this particular meditation, remember or create the feeling of coming home and feeling released from external pressures. This is a place and time for you to be just as you wish. The less expectations you have of the meditation, the easier it will be for the inner world to reveal itself to you; so simply sit and be....

Meditation: A MOTHER LOVE

ENTER the temple of meditation and prayer, losing all sense of separateness…. Merge into the eternal Love, which enfolds all living souls, for we are one….

Words cannot fully describe the heavenly life. You live in a material world of a very heavy vibration; but just for this time, close your eyes to all that is crude and harsh, and visualize, on the altar, the beauty of a rose. See not only the form, but the vibrant life-force which issues forth….

Then transmute your rose into a light—golden light—so bright and beautiful that the physical eye flinches from it. Will you feel the essence, the perfume from such a flower? Even then you touch only the very outermost fringe of its indwelling life, which is called 'God', from whom you also emanate and to whom you will return.

Keep in your mind this picture of light, indwelling sweetness and purity, symbolized in the best way we know—as a rose, a flower sweet and beautiful….

As you gaze upon the rose, breathe in the essence of God. Become permeated with the God-life. You are in the heart of Love. Open wide the channel of your being to the outpouring of divine love, wisdom and power.

A great Mother Love holds all in Her arms, and you know only love; you know that God is good, you know that all moves forward to a perfect and glorious realization.

And so the strength of spirit dwells with you and leads you upward and onward to God, and the fire of God's life will grow in power and radiance within your heart.

May you ever be mindful of your true nature.

'Go your way holding in your heart the image of the joy of the dear Lord Jesus, and the purity of his touch. All people can be servers, healers. All can be consolers. What a lovely word—to *console* your brother, your sister! What more beautiful task can you be given? Humbly thank your Creator for this precious gift and for the opportunity to use it. To be a servant of God is the most lovely gift that may be given to you all.'